CONTENTS

Downloadable Maps

Ten maps used in this book are available for download on our Web site, as well as two color maps: one projection map of the world and one political map of Africa.

How to Download:

1. Go to www.evan-moor.com/resources.
2. Enter your e-mail address and the resource code for this product—EMC3737.
3. You will receive an e-mail with a link to the downloadable maps.

What's in This Book

▶ **5 sections** of reproducible information and activity pages centered on five main topics: Africa in the World, Political Divisions, Physical Features, Valuable Resources, and Culture

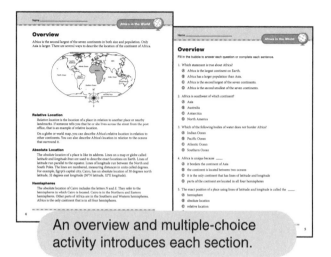

An overview and multiple-choice activity introduces each section.

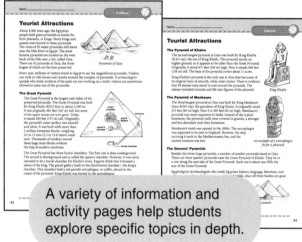

A variety of information and activity pages help students explore specific topics in depth.

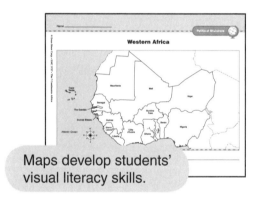

Maps develop students' visual literacy skills.

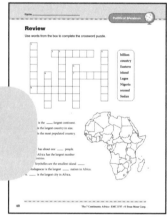

A crossword puzzle at the end of each section provides a fun review activity.

▶ **1 section** of assessment activities

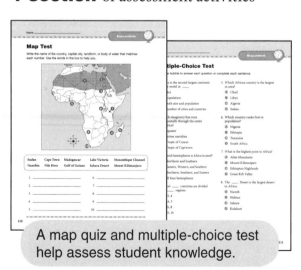

A map quiz and multiple-choice test help assess student knowledge.

▶ **1 section** of open-ended note takers

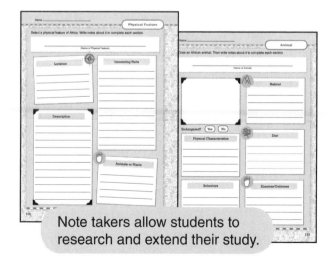

Note takers allow students to research and extend their study.

Africa in the World

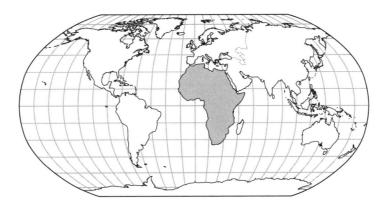

This section introduces students to the location of Africa in the world. Students learn about the difference between relative and absolute location, as well as the hemispheres in which Africa lies. Students also practice using lines of latitude and longitude to find places on a map.

Each skill in this section is based on the following National Geography Standards:

Essential Element 1: The World in Spatial Terms

Standard 1: How to use maps and other geographic representations, tools, and technologies to acquire, process, and report information from a spatial perspective

CONTENTS

Overview

Africa is the second largest of the seven continents in both size and population. Only Asia is larger. There are several ways to describe the location of the continent of Africa.

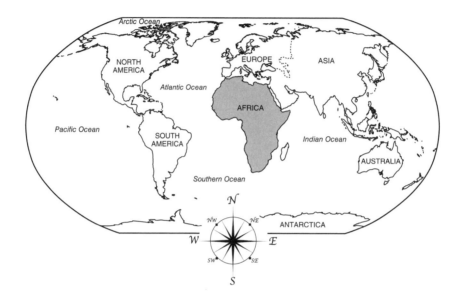

Relative Location

Relative location is the location of a place in relation to another place or nearby landmarks. If someone tells you that he or she lives across the street from the post office, that is an example of relative location.

On a globe or world map, you can describe Africa's relative location in relation to other continents. You can also describe Africa's location in relation to the oceans that surround it.

Absolute Location

The *absolute location* of a place is like its address. Lines on a map or globe called *latitude* and *longitude lines* are used to describe exact locations on Earth. Lines of latitude run parallel to the equator. Lines of longitude run between the North and South Poles. The lines are numbered, measuring distances in units called degrees. For example, Egypt's capital city, Cairo, has an absolute location of 30 degrees north latitude, 32 degrees east longitude (30°N latitude, 32°E longitude).

Hemispheres

The absolute location of Cairo includes the letters *N* and *E*. They refer to the hemispheres in which Cairo is located. Cairo is in the Northern and Eastern hemispheres. Other parts of Africa are in the Southern and Western hemispheres. Africa is the only continent that is in all four hemispheres.

Overview

Fill in the bubble to answer each question or complete each sentence.

1. Which statement is true about Africa?

Ⓐ Africa is the largest continent on Earth.

Ⓑ Africa has a larger population than Asia.

Ⓒ Africa is the second largest of the seven continents.

Ⓓ Africa is the second smallest of the seven continents.

2. Africa is southwest of which continent?

Ⓐ Asia

Ⓑ Australia

Ⓒ Antarctica

Ⓓ North America

3. Which of the following bodies of water does *not* border Africa?

Ⓐ Indian Ocean

Ⓑ Pacific Ocean

Ⓒ Atlantic Ocean

Ⓓ Southern Ocean

4. Africa is unique because _____.

Ⓐ it borders the continent of Asia

Ⓑ the continent is located between two oceans

Ⓒ it is the only continent that has lines of latitude and longitude

Ⓓ parts of the continent are located in all four hemispheres

5. The exact position of a place using lines of latitude and longitude is called the _____.

Ⓐ hemisphere

Ⓑ absolute location

Ⓒ relative location

Ⓓ intermediate direction

Africa's Relative Location

Relative location is the position of a place in relation to another place. How would you describe where Africa is located in the world using relative location?

Look at the world map on the other page. One way to describe Africa's relative location is to name the other continents that border it. For example, Africa is south of Europe and northeast of South America.

Another way to describe the relative location of Africa is to name the oceans that surround the continent. For example, Africa is west of the Indian Ocean and east of the Atlantic Ocean.

A. Use the map on the other page to complete the paragraph about the relative location of Africa.

Africa is the second-largest continent in the world. It is located south

of the continent of _____. Africa is north of

_____, the coldest continent. Northeast of Africa

is the large continent of _____. To the southwest

of Africa is the continent of _____.

Two oceans border Africa. To the west is the _____

Ocean. The Indian Ocean is _____ of Africa. The

_____ Sea forms a northeast border between Africa and

Asia. The larger _____ Sea separates Africa from Europe.

B. Follow the directions to color the map on the other page.

1. Color the continent directly north of Africa red.

2. Use blue to circle the name of the ocean that is west of Africa.

3. Draw a panda on the large continent northeast of Africa.

The 7 Continents: Africa • EMC 3737 • © Evan-Moor Corp.

Name _____

Africa's Relative Location

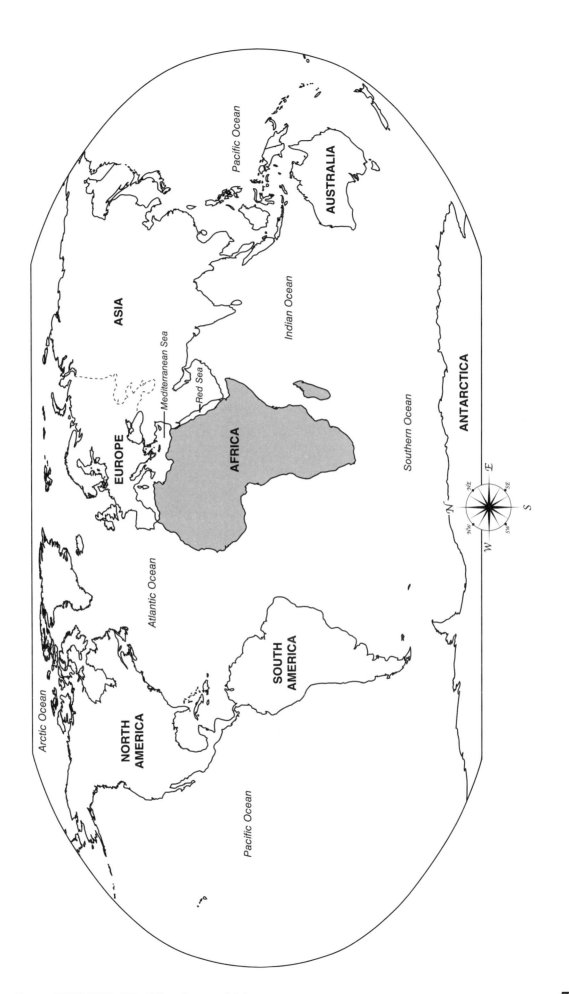

Africa's Hemispheres

On a globe, Earth is divided into four hemispheres by a horizontal line called the *equator* and by vertical lines that run from the North Pole to the South Pole. The hemispheres are the Northern, Southern, Western, and Eastern. Africa is part of both the Northern and Southern hemispheres because the equator runs through the middle of the continent. Africa is mostly located in the Eastern Hemisphere, but part of the "bulge" of Africa is in the Western Hemisphere.

Northern and Southern Hemispheres

A globe shows an imaginary horizontal line that runs around the center of Earth. This line is called the equator. The equator divides Earth into the Northern and Southern hemispheres.

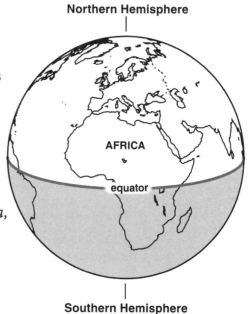

Since the equator runs through Africa, the continent is located in both the Northern and Southern hemispheres.

Western and Eastern Hemispheres

A globe also shows imaginary vertical lines that run from the North Pole to the South Pole. One of these lines is called the *prime meridian*. This line, along with its twin line on the opposite side of the globe, create the Western and Eastern hemispheres.

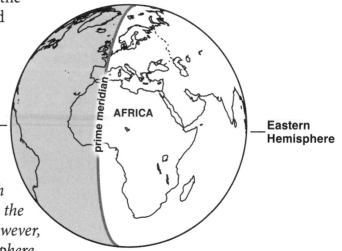

Since the prime meridian runs through Africa, the continent is located in both the Eastern and Western hemispheres. However, most of Africa is in the Eastern Hemisphere.

Africa's Hemispheres

A. Write the letter of the definition that matches each term. Use the information and pictures of the globes on the other page to help you.

_____ 1. Africa

_____ 2. continent

_____ 3. globe

_____ 4. equator

_____ 5. Northern Hemisphere

_____ 6. hemisphere

_____ 7. prime meridian

_____ 8. Southern Hemisphere

_____ 9. Eastern Hemisphere

a. an imaginary line that runs from the North Pole to the South Pole

b. half of Earth

c. the continent that is located in all four hemispheres

d. the hemisphere that is east of the prime meridian

e. an imaginary line that divides Earth into the Northern and Southern hemispheres

f. any of the seven large landmasses of Earth

g. the hemisphere that is south of the equator

h. a round model of Earth

i. the hemisphere that is north of the equator

B. Label the parts of the globe. Use the letters next to the terms in the box.

A. Southern Hemisphere

B. Africa

C. Northern Hemisphere

D. Eastern Hemisphere

E. equator

F. prime meridian

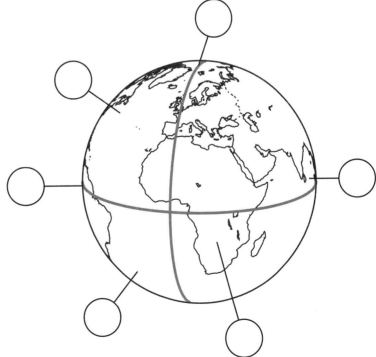

Africa's Absolute Location

Many globes contain lines that make it easier to find specific places on Earth. Lines of latitude measure the distance north and south of the equator. Lines of longitude measure the distance east and west of the prime meridian. You can use lines of latitude and longitude to find the absolute location of Africa on a globe.

Latitude

The equator is found at the absolute location of 0° (zero degrees) latitude. Other lines of latitude run parallel to the equator and are labeled with an *N* or *S*, depending on whether they are north or south of the equator. Latitude lines are also called *parallels*.

On the picture of the globe, notice the lines of latitude. Look for the continent of Africa. Since the equator runs through the middle of Africa, half of the latitude lines used to find the absolute location of places in Africa are labeled in *degrees north*, or *°N*, and half are labeled in *degrees south*, or *°S*.

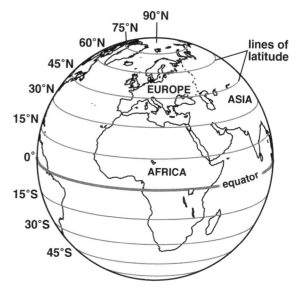

Lines of Latitude (Parallels)

Longitude

The prime meridian runs from the North Pole to the South Pole at 0° (zero degrees) longitude. Other lines of longitude run north and south, too, and are labeled with an *E* or *W*, depending on whether they are east or west of the prime meridian. Longitude lines are also called *meridians*.

On the picture of the globe, notice the lines of longitude. Look for the continent of Africa. Since most of the continent is east of the prime meridian, most of the longitude lines used to find the absolute location of places in Africa are labeled in *degrees east*, or *°E*. Some parts of the continent are west of the prime meridian. The absolute location of those parts are labeled in *degrees west*, or *°W*.

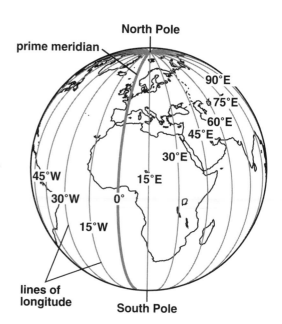

Lines of Longitude (Meridians)

Name _____

Africa's Absolute Location

To find the absolute location of a place, read the latitude line first and then read the longitude line. For example, the latitude 30°N runs through the northern part of Africa in the country of Egypt. The longitude 30°E runs through the eastern part of Africa, including the eastern part of Egypt. So the absolute location of the northeastern part of Egypt is 30°N latitude, 30°E longitude.

A. Circle the correct answer to each question. Use the pictures of the globes and information on the other page to help you.

1. Which line is at 0 degrees latitude?	**equator**	**prime meridian**
2. Which line runs north and south?	**equator**	**prime meridian**
3. Which line runs through the center of Africa?	**equator**	**prime meridian**
4. Which line of longitude runs through the center of Africa?	**15°E**	**15°W**
5. Where is the North Pole located?	**90°S**	**90°N**
6. Which lines run parallel to the equator?	**latitude lines**	**longitude lines**
7. How many degrees are between each line of latitude and longitude on the globes?	**10 degrees**	**15 degrees**
8. What is another name for lines of latitude?	**meridians**	**parallels**
9. Which line of latitude runs through Africa?	**30°S**	**60°S**
10. What is another name for lines of longitude?	**parallels**	**meridians**

B. Using the information on this page and the other page, explain why Egypt has an absolute location labeled in degrees north and east.

_____

_____

Using a Projection Map

How do you draw a picture of a round object, such as Earth, on a flat piece of paper? In order to show all of Earth's continents and oceans in one view, mapmakers use a system called *projection*. Mapping the round Earth on a flat surface causes some areas to look bigger than they really are. For example, land near the poles gets stretched out when flattened. That's why Greenland and Antarctica look so big on some maps.

A projection map of the world shows all the lines of latitude and longitude on Earth. Study the projection map on the other page. Notice the lines of latitude and longitude. You can use these lines to find the absolute location of a specific place in Africa. For example, the first *A* in the label *Africa* is located at 7°N latitude, 15°E longitude.

A. Read each statement. Circle **yes** if it is true or **no** if it is false. Use the map on the other page to help you.

1. The prime meridian runs through Africa.   **Yes** **No**

2. The equator runs through the middle of Africa.   **Yes** **No**

3. All of Africa is located between the latitudes of 30°N and 30°S.   **Yes** **No**

4. Most of Africa is east of the prime meridian.   **Yes** **No**

5. The absolute location 15°S latitude, 30°E longitude is in Africa.   **Yes** **No**

6. The absolute location 45°N latitude, 60°E longitude is in Africa.   **Yes** **No**

7. The large island off the southeast coast of mainland Africa   **Yes** **No**
   has an absolute location of 15°N latitude, 60°E longitude.

8. Africa shares the latitude line of 30°S with Australia and   **Yes** **No**
   South America.

B. How many continents can you find on the map that share the longitude line of 15°E? Write their names.

_____

_____

Name _____

Using a Projection Map

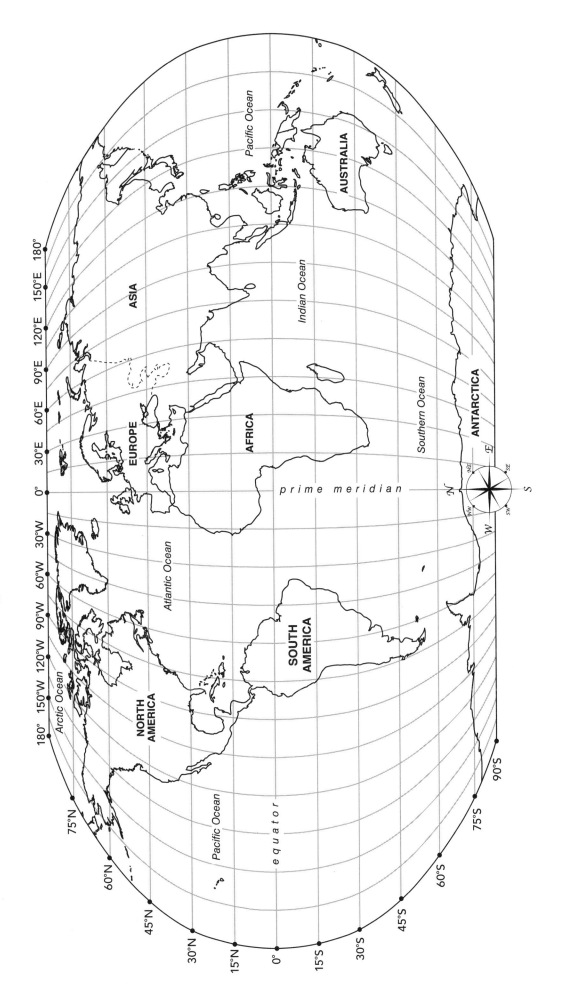

Review

Use words from the box to complete the crossword puzzle.

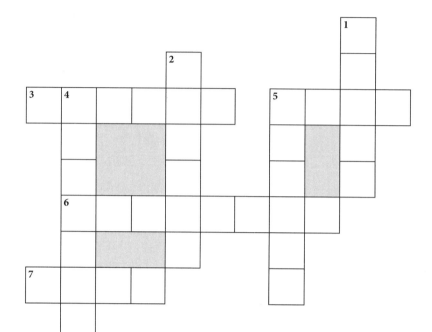

Africa
Asia
Atlantic
equator
four
Indian
prime
second

Across

3. Africa is the ____ largest of the seven continents.

5. Africa is southwest of the large continent of ____.

6. The ____ Ocean borders Africa to the west.

7. Africa is located in ____ hemispheres.

Down

1. The ____ meridian divides the Earth into the Eastern and Western hemispheres.

2. The ____ Ocean is east of Africa.

4. The imaginary line that runs through the center of Africa is called the ____.

5. Most of ____ is located in the Eastern Hemisphere.

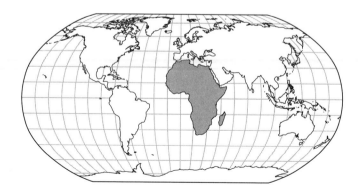

Political Divisions of Africa

This section introduces students to the five regions and 54 countries of Africa. Students learn how the regions differ in size by studying data about the largest and smallest countries by area. Students also discover which countries and cities in Africa are the most populated.

Each skill in this section is based on the following National Geography Standards:

Essential Element 2: Places and Regions

Standard 5: People create regions to interpret Earth's complexity

Essential Element 4: Human Systems

Standard 9: The characteristics, distribution, and migration of human populations on Earth's surface

CONTENTS

Overview

Africa is the second-largest continent in both size and population.

- Africa covers about 20% of the world's landmass.

- About 20% of the world's population—or 1 billion people—live in Africa.

- Africa has 54 countries. That's more than any other continent.

The Five Regions

The 54 countries of Africa are divided into five regions.

Region	Number of Countries	Fast Facts
Northern Africa	7	bordered by the Mediterranean and Red seas
Western Africa	16	has the most populated country—Nigeria
Central Africa	9	also called Middle Africa
Eastern Africa	17	has the largest island nation—Madagascar
Southern Africa	5	contains the southernmost country—South Africa

These political regions are designated by the United Nations. Other sources may divide the regions differently.

Where People Live

About two-thirds of all Africans live in rural areas or villages. However, throughout Africa, more and more rural people are moving to the cities for work. Usually, it is the young men who leave their villages to work in the city in order to support their family members who stay in the villages.

Many of Africa's cities are densely populated, meaning they have a large number of people in each square mile (or kilometer). In Cairo, Egypt, there are approximately 94,000 people per square mile (36,000 per square km). The cities of Lagos, Nigeria, and Kinshasa, Democratic Republic of the Congo, are also greatly overcrowded.

Population experts predict that by 2050, the world will have 9 billion people. Of that 9 billion, 2 billion will be living in Africa.

Overview

Fill in the bubble to answer each question or complete each sentence.

1. Africa has _____ countries that are divided into _____ regions.
   - Ⓐ 5, 54
   - Ⓑ 20, 20
   - Ⓒ 54, 5
   - Ⓓ 54, 6

2. Which region of Africa has the most countries?
   - Ⓐ Northern Africa
   - Ⓑ Southern Africa
   - Ⓒ Western Africa
   - Ⓓ Eastern Africa

3. Most Africans live in _____.
   - Ⓐ cities
   - Ⓑ rural areas
   - Ⓒ desert areas
   - Ⓓ southern Africa

4. Which of these large cities was *not* mentioned in the overview?
   - Ⓐ Cairo, Egypt
   - Ⓑ Lagos, Nigeria
   - Ⓒ Cape Town, South Africa
   - Ⓓ Kinshasa, Democratic Republic of the Congo

5. Which statement is true about Africa?
   - Ⓐ Africa is the second-largest continent in both size and population.
   - Ⓑ Africa is the third-largest continent in both size and population.
   - Ⓒ About one-half of the people of Africa live in densely populated cities.
   - Ⓓ By 2050, experts predict that Africa will be the largest continent in the world.

Population of Africa

A *population census* is a survey by a national government to gather information about the number of people who live in that country. Population censuses have been taken since ancient times. The earliest known population counts were made by the Chinese and Egyptians. Today, countries conduct an official census every 10 years. Experts look at the population figures from the past and present and try to predict what the population will be in the future.

Throughout modern history, Africa has had the second-largest population of all the continents. Only Asia has more people. In 1950, Africa's population was about 228 million. By 2010, the population had grown to about 1 billion. Africa's population is expected to continue growing steadily, reaching 2 billion by 2050.

Africa's Population: 1950–2050

Year	Population (actual)	Population (rounded to nearest million)
1950	227,939,046	228 million
1970	365,897,577	366 million
1990	633,224,161	633 million
2010	1,016,511,552	1 billion (1,017 million)
2030	1,507,900,283	1.5 billion (1,508 million)
2050	2,073,016,270	2.1 billion (2,073 million)

A. Look at the chart above. Do you think it is reasonable to predict that Africa's population might increase to 2.5 billion by 2070? Why or why not?

_____

_____

_____

Population of Africa

B. Read each statement. Circle **yes** if it is true or **no** if it is false. Use the information on the other page to help you.

1. The chart shows population growth over a 100-year period.   **Yes**   **No**

2. In 1950, Africa had a population of almost 228 million.   **Yes**   **No**

3. In 1990, the population of Africa reached 1 billion.   **Yes**   **No**

4. From 1950 to 1990, Africa's population increased by about 405 million.   **Yes**   **No**

5. In 1970, Africa's population was 365,897,577.   **Yes**   **No**

6. Projections show that Africa will have a population of 2 billion in 2030.   **Yes**   **No**

7. From 2030 to 2050, Africa's population will decrease by 500 million.   **Yes**   **No**

8. The chart shows population growth figures in 20-year segments.   **Yes**   **No**

9. The smallest population increase took place between the years 1990 and 2010.   **Yes**   **No**

10. The chart suggests that by 2040, Africa's population will be decreasing.   **Yes**   **No**

C. Using the rounded population figures in the chart on the other page, circle the population increase that occurred between 1950 and 2010.

72 million   **772 million**   **1.77 billion**

Countries of Africa

Read and say the names of the countries, using the pronunciations to help you. Look at the map of Africa on the other page to see where the countries are located.

Algeria
(al-JEER-ee-uh)

Angola
(an-GOAL-uh)

Benin
(buh-NIN)

Botswana
(baht-SWAN-uh)

Burkina Faso
(bur-KEEN-uh
FAH-soh)

Burundi
(buh-ROON-dee)

Cameroon
(kam-uh-ROON)

Cape Verde
(cape vurd)

Central African Republic

Chad

Comoros
(KAHM-uh-roze)

Côte d'Ivoire
(KOAT dih-VWAR)

**Democratic Republic
of the Congo**

Djibouti
(jih-BOOT-ee)

Egypt
(EE-jipt)

Equatorial Guinea
(EE-kwah-TOR-ee-ul GIH-nee)

Eritrea
(AIR-ih-TREE-uh)

Ethiopia
(EE-thee-OH-pee-uh)

Gabon
(gah-BONE)

Gambia, The
(GAM-bee-uh)

Ghana
(GAH-nuh)

Guinea
(GIH-nee)

Guinea-Bissau
(GIH-nee bih-SOW)

Kenya
(KEN-yuh)

Lesotho
(leh-SOH-toh)

Liberia
(lye-BEER-ee-uh)

Libya
(LIH-bee-uh)

Madagascar
(MAD-uh-GAS-kur)

Malawi
(mah-LAH-wee)

Mali
(MAH-lee)

Mauritania
(MAWR-uh-TAY-nee-uh)

Mauritius
(maw-RIH-shus)

Morocco
(muh-RAH-koh)

Mozambique
(MOE-zahm-BEEK)

Namibia
(nuh-MIH-bee-uh)

Niger
(NYE-jur)

Nigeria
(nye-JEER-ee-uh)

Republic of the Congo

Republic of South Sudan
(soo-DAN)

Rwanda
(ruh-WAHN-duh)

São Tomé and Príncipe
(SOW toh-MAY and
PREEN-sih-pay)

Senegal
(SEH-nih-gawl)

Seychelles
(say-SHELLZ)

Sierra Leone
(see-AIR-uh lee-OWN)

Somalia
(soh-MAH-lee-uh)

South Africa

Sudan
(soo-DAN)

Swaziland
(SWAH-zee-land)

Tanzania
(TAN-zuh-NEE-uh)

Togo
(TOH-goh)

Tunisia
(too-NEE-zhuh)

Uganda
(yoo-GAHN-dah)

Zambia
(ZAM-bee-uh)

Zimbabwe
(zim-BAHB-way)

Name _____

Countries of Africa

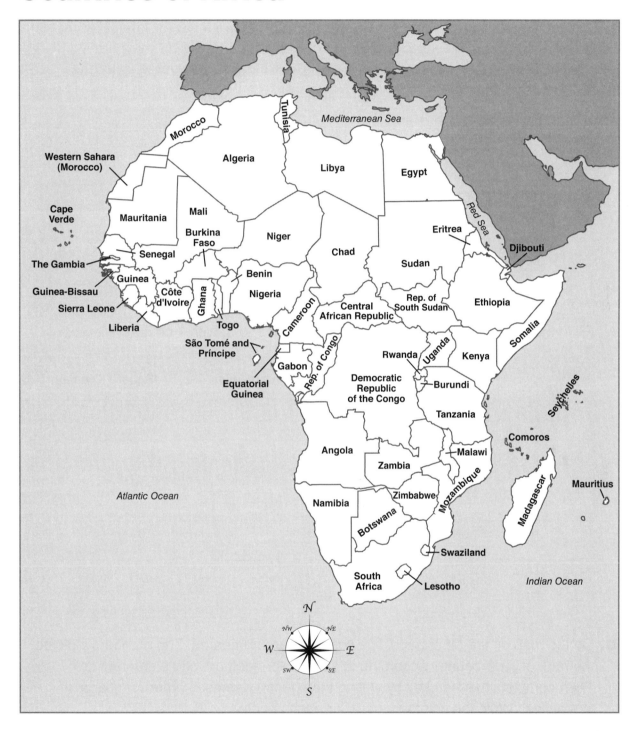

Largest Countries by Area

Africa has several countries that are large in terms of square miles (or kilometers). However, Africa's largest countries are still not as big as countries on some other continents. For example, the largest country in Africa is less than one-quarter the size of the United States.

The five largest countries of Africa (listed in alphabetical order) are:

Algeria: 919,595 square miles (2,381,741 square km)

Chad: 496,000 square miles (1,284,000 square km)

DRC*: 905,355 square miles (2,344,858 square km)

Libya: 679,360 square miles (1,759,540 square km)

Sudan: 718,720 square miles (1,861,484 square km)

*This is the commonly-used abbreviation for the Democratic Republic of the Congo.

A. Fill in the chart to rank the countries in size from **1** to **5**, with **1** being the largest.

Rank in Size	Country	Square Miles	Square Kilometers
1			
2			
3			
4			
5			

B. On the map on the other page, five countries are numbered. The numbers indicate the rank of each country according to size. Color each country a different color. Then complete the map key by writing the country names in order from largest to smallest. Write the color you used for each country.

Name _____

Largest Countries by Area

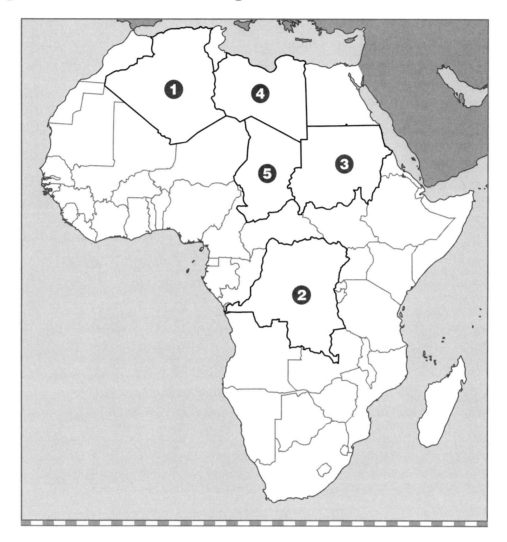

MAP KEY

The Five Largest Countries	Color
1. _____	_____
2. _____	_____
3. _____	_____
4. _____	_____
5. _____	_____

Smallest Countries by Area

The smallest countries in Africa are all island nations. Each nation is an *archipelago*, or group of islands, and is made up of larger main islands and a number of smaller islands.

The five smallest countries of Africa (listed in alphabetical order) are:

Cape Verde: 1,557 square miles (4,033 square km), 10 main islands

Comoros: 719 square miles (1,862 square km), 3 main islands

Mauritius: 788 square miles (2,040 square km), 1 main island

São Tomé and Príncipe: 372 square miles (964 square km), 2 main islands

Seychelles: 176 square miles (455 square km), 3 main islands

A. Fill in the chart to rank the countries in size from **1** to **5**, with **1** being the smallest. Also include the number of main islands for each country.

Rank in Size	Country	Square Miles	Square Kilometers	Number of Main Islands
1				
2				
3				
4				
5				

B. On the map on the other page, five countries are numbered. The numbers indicate the rank of each country according to size. Color each country a different color. Then complete the map key by writing the country names in order from smallest to largest. Write the color you used for each country.

The 7 Continents: Africa • EMC 3737 • © Evan-Moor Corp.

Smallest Countries by Area

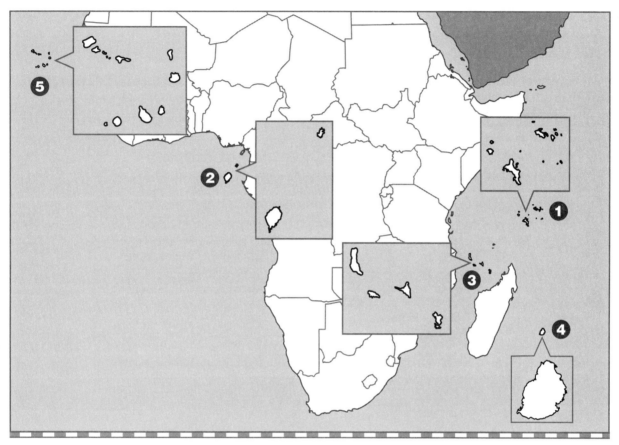

This map of Africa does not show all the islands that make up each country.

MAP KEY

The Five Smallest Countries	Color
1. _____	_____
2. _____	_____
3. _____	_____
4. _____	_____
5. _____	_____

Largest Countries by Population

Africa is a continent that has 12 of the 50 most populated countries in the world. Nigeria, the country with the largest population in Africa, is the eighth most populated country in the world.

Two ways to read large numbers are by standard form and by word form. For example, 150,274,000 is written in standard form. In word form, the number is written out like this: 150 million, 274 thousand.

Most Populated Countries of Africa

	Country	Population
1	Nigeria	152,217,000 (152 million, 217 thousand)
2	Ethiopia	88,013,000 (88 million, 13 thousand)
3	Egypt	80,472,000 (80 million, 472 thousand)
4	Congo, Democratic Republic of the	70,916,000 (70 million, 916 thousand)
5	South Africa	49,109,000 (49 million, 109 thousand)
6	Tanzania	41,893,000 (41 million, 893 thousand)
7	Kenya	40,047,000 (40 million, 47 thousand)
8	Sudan	34,848,000 (34 million, 848 thousand)
9	Algeria	34,586,000 (34 million, 586 thousand)
10	Uganda	33,399,000 (33 million, 339 thousand)
11	Morocco	31,627,000 (31 million, 627 thousand)
12	Ghana	24,340,000 (24 million, 340 thousand)

Populations are 2010 estimates based on figures from the U.S. Census Bureau, International Database.

Largest Countries by Population

A. Look at the chart on the other page. Notice that the population figures are written in both standard form and word form. Use the information in the chart to answer the questions below.

1. How many countries have a population of over 100,000,000? _____

2. Which country has a population of 80 million, 472 thousand? _____

3. How many countries have a population of under 50 million? _____

4. Which country has a population of 88,013,000? _____

5. Which country has a population that is about half of Egypt's population? _____

6. Which countries rank 1st and 12th in population?

   1st: _____   12th: _____

7. Write the population of Tanzania in word form.

   _____

8. What is the fifth-largest country in Africa? Write its name and population in word form.

   _____

B. When reading the chart on the other page, remember that population figures are always changing. Go to the U.S. Census Bureau Website to see the second-by-second population clocks. As of the day this was written, the U.S. population was 309,008,002 and changing every second. The world population was 6,812,963,410.

   What is the U.S. population right now?   _____

   What is the world population right now?   _____

Northern Africa

Northern Africa is a region made up of seven countries. They are Algeria, Egypt, Libya, Morocco, Republic of South Sudan, Sudan, and Tunisia. Western Sahara is also part of this region and is considered to be a territory mostly belonging to Morocco. The Mediterranean and Red seas border Northern Africa and help to separate the region from the continents of Asia and Europe.

In Northern Africa, Algeria is the largest country in size, and Tunisia is the smallest. Northern Africa has a total population of about 206 million. Egypt is the most populated country in the region. Cairo, the capital of Egypt, is the largest city in Northern Africa and the second-largest city on the entire continent.

A. Complete each sentence by unscrambling the word under the line. Use the map of Northern Africa on the other page and the information above to help you.

1. Northern Africa is made up of seven _____.
                                                    secirotun

2. Northern Africa has about 206 _____ people.
                                          nomilil

3. The country of _____ has the largest population.
                          ptyge

4. The country of _____ is the largest in size.
                      largeai

5. The largest city in Northern Africa is _____.
                                                  airco

6. An area called _____ is part of Northern Africa.
                    nretsew ashaar

7. _____ is the smallest country.
        tiasinu

8. Northern Africa is separated from Asia and Europe by the Red and

_____ seas.
    nterraeanidem

B. On the map on the other page, color each country and the territory of Western Sahara a different color.

Northern Africa

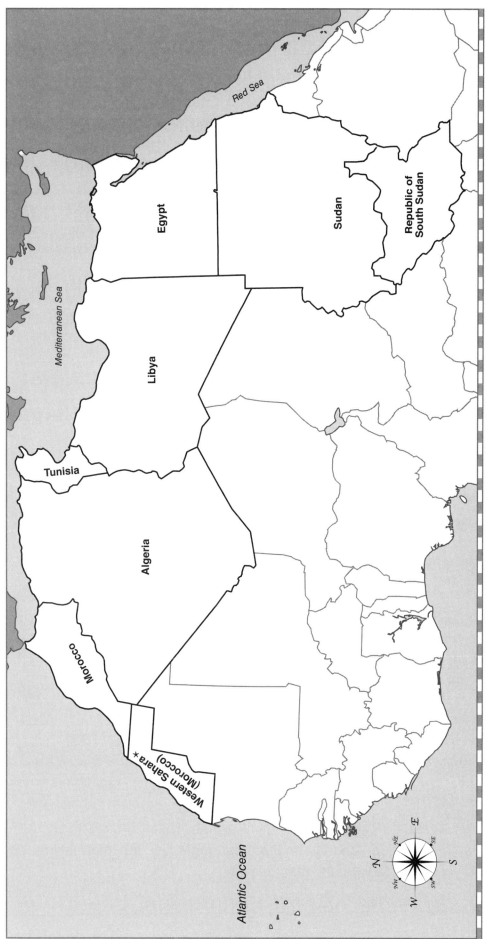

Mediterranean Sea

Red Sea

Egypt

Sudan

Republic of
South Sudan

Libya

Tunisia

Algeria

Morocco

Western Sahara *
(Morocco)

Atlantic Ocean

*As of the date this book was published, Western Sahara was not recognized as an independent country by the U.S. State Department.

Name _____

Western Africa

The region of Western Africa is made up of 16 countries. They are Benin, Burkina Faso, Cape Verde, Côte d'Ivoire, The Gambia, Ghana, Guinea, Guinea-Bissau, Liberia, Mali, Mauritania, Niger, Nigeria, Senegal, Sierra Leone, and Togo. The Atlantic Ocean forms the western and southern borders of the region.

The smallest country in Western Africa is Cape Verde, an island nation. Niger is the largest country in the region. Just south of Niger is the country of Nigeria, which has the largest population not only of Western Africa, but of the whole continent. Lagos, the capital of Nigeria, is the most populated city in all of Africa.

A. Read each statement. Circle **yes** if it is true or **no** if it is false. Use the map on the other page and the information above to help you.

1. There are 18 countries in Western Africa.   **Yes**   **No**

2. Cape Verde is the smallest island nation in Western Africa.   **Yes**   **No**

3. The Indian Ocean borders the region to the west and to the south.   **Yes**   **No**

4. Nigeria has the largest population in the region.   **Yes**   **No**

5. The most populated city in all of Africa is located in Western Africa.   **Yes**   **No**

6. Ghana is bordered by Burkina Faso, Liberia, and Togo.   **Yes**   **No**

7. Mali, Mauritania, and Niger are the northernmost countries in the region.   **Yes**   **No**

8. Four countries and an ocean border Liberia.   **Yes**   **No**

9. Guinea is larger in area than Guinea-Bissau.   **Yes**   **No**

10. Most of The Gambia is surrounded by Senegal.   **Yes**   **No**

B. Write a caption under the map on the other page. Use the information above to help you describe what the map shows.

Name _____

Western Africa

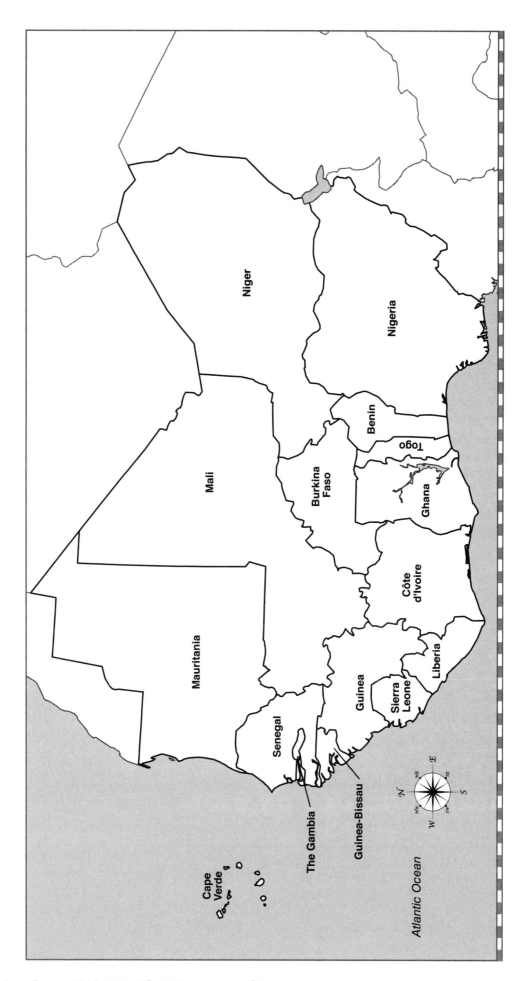

Mauritania

Mali

Niger

Nigeria

Benin

Togo

Burkina Faso

Ghana

Côte d'Ivoire

Senegal

The Gambia

Guinea-Bissau

Guinea

Sierra Leone

Liberia

Cape Verde

Atlantic Ocean

N
NW NE
W E
SW SE
S

Central Africa

Central Africa, or Middle Africa, is made up of nine countries. All but two of the nine countries—Chad and the Central African Republic—are located along the western coast.

Countries of Central Africa

Country	Square Miles (square km)	Population
Angola	481,351 square miles (1,246,700 square km)	13,068,161
Cameroon	183,568 square miles (475,440 square km)	19,294,149
Central African Republic	240,535 square miles (622,984 square km)	4,578,768
Chad	495,755 square miles (1,284,000 square km)	10,543,464
Democratic Republic of the Congo	905,355 square miles (2,344,858 square km)	70,916,439
Equatorial Guinea	10,831 square miles (28,051 square km)	650,702
Gabon	103,347 square miles (267,667 square km)	1,545,255
Republic of the Congo	132,047 square miles (342,000 square km)	4,124,339
São Tomé and Príncipe	372 square miles (964 square km)	219,334

Answer the questions below, using the information above and the map on the other page to help you.

1. Which country is the largest in size? _____

2. What is another name for Central Africa? _____

3. Which country is the smallest in population? _____

4. Which country's area is 183,568 square miles? _____

5. Which country is the farthest north in the region? _____

Central Africa

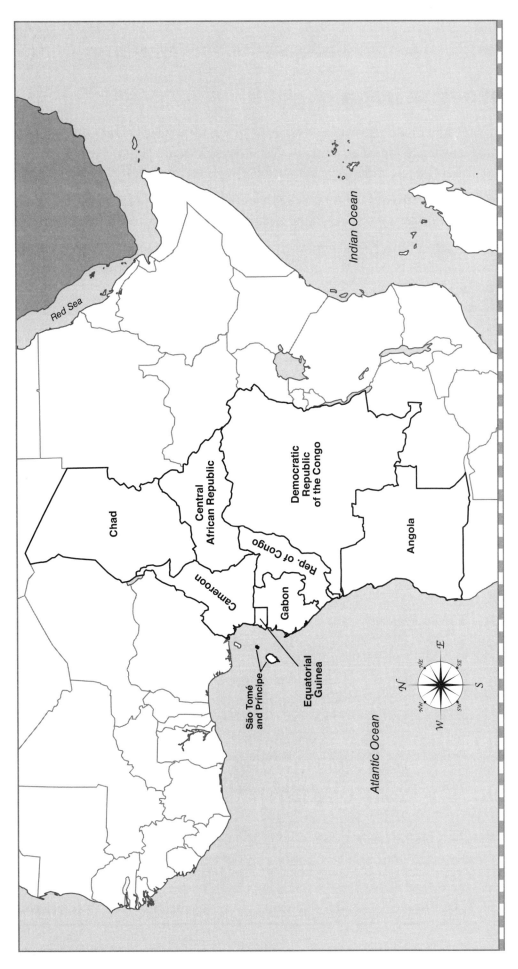

Red Sea

Indian Ocean

Chad

Central
African Republic

Democratic
Republic
of the Congo

Cameroon

Rep. of Congo

Gabon

Angola

São Tomé
and Príncipe

Equatorial
Guinea

Atlantic Ocean

N

NE

NW

E

SE

W

SW

S

Eastern Africa

Eastern Africa is made up of 17 countries. They are Burundi, Comoros, Djibouti, Eritrea, Ethiopia, Kenya, Madagascar, Malawi, Mauritius, Mozambique, Rwanda, Seychelles, Somalia, Tanzania, Uganda, Zambia, and Zimbabwe.

The countries of Eritrea, Ethiopia, Somalia, and Djibouti are located in an area called the *Horn of Africa.* It was given this name because the land is shaped like a rhinoceros's horn.

Eastern Africa has both the largest and smallest island nations in Africa. Madagascar is the largest, and Seychelles is the smallest. The other island nations in the region are Comoros and Mauritius.

The three largest countries in Eastern Africa are, in order, Ethiopia, Tanzania, and Mozambique. The three most populated countries in the region are Ethiopia, Tanzania, and Kenya. The largest city in Eastern Africa is Addis Ababa, which is the capital of Ethiopia. Nairobi, Kenya, is the second-largest city.

A. Write the letter of the description that matches each place name. Use the map on the other page and the information above to help you.

_____ 1. Addis Ababa

_____ 2. Eastern Africa

_____ 3. Ethiopia

_____ 4. Horn of Africa

_____ 5. Madagascar

_____ 6. Indian Ocean

_____ 7. Seychelles

_____ 8. Tanzania

a. a region of 17 African countries

b. the second-largest country in both size and population

c. a body of water that borders Eastern Africa

d. the largest island nation

e. the smallest island nation

f. the countries of Eritrea, Ethiopia, Somalia, and Djibouti make up this area

g. the largest country in both size and population

h. the most populated city of Eastern Africa

B. On the map on the other page, color each of the following countries a different color. Under the map, write one fact about each of these countries.

| Ethiopia | Madagascar | Seychelles | Tanzania |

Eastern Africa

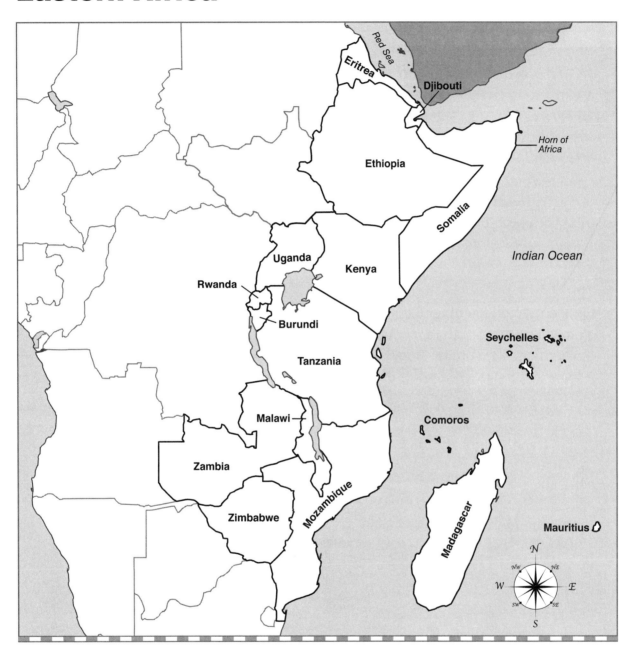

Ethiopia: _____

Madagascar: _____

Seychelles: _____

Tanzania: _____

Southern Africa

The region of Southern Africa is made up of five countries. They are Botswana, Lesotho, Namibia, South Africa, and Swaziland.

South Africa is the largest country in the region in both size and population. It is 470,693 square miles (1,219,090 square km). That's almost twice the size of the state of Texas. South Africa has more than 49 million people, nearly twice as many as Texas. The country with the next-largest population in Southern Africa is Lesotho, and it has only a little more than 2 million people.

The smallest country in the region, in both size and population, is Swaziland. It is only 6,704 square miles (17,364 square km) and has just 1.3 million people. Swaziland and Lesotho both lie entirely within the larger country of South Africa, even though they are independent countries.

A. The chart below shows the capital cities of the five Southern African countries. On the map on the other page, write the name of each capital next to the correct star. Notice that South Africa has three capital cities, one for each branch of government. Two are labeled on the map. Label the third one.

Country	Capital
Botswana	Gaborone
Lesotho	Maseru
Namibia	Windhoek
South Africa	Pretoria (executive branch) Bloemfontein (judicial branch) Cape Town (legislative branch)
Swaziland	Mbabane

B. Answer the questions below, using the map on the other page to help you. Then follow the directions to color the map.

1. Which country in Southern Africa has its coastline _____ entirely on the Atlantic Ocean? Color it yellow.

2. Which large country does *not* have a coastline? _____ Color it green.

Southern Africa

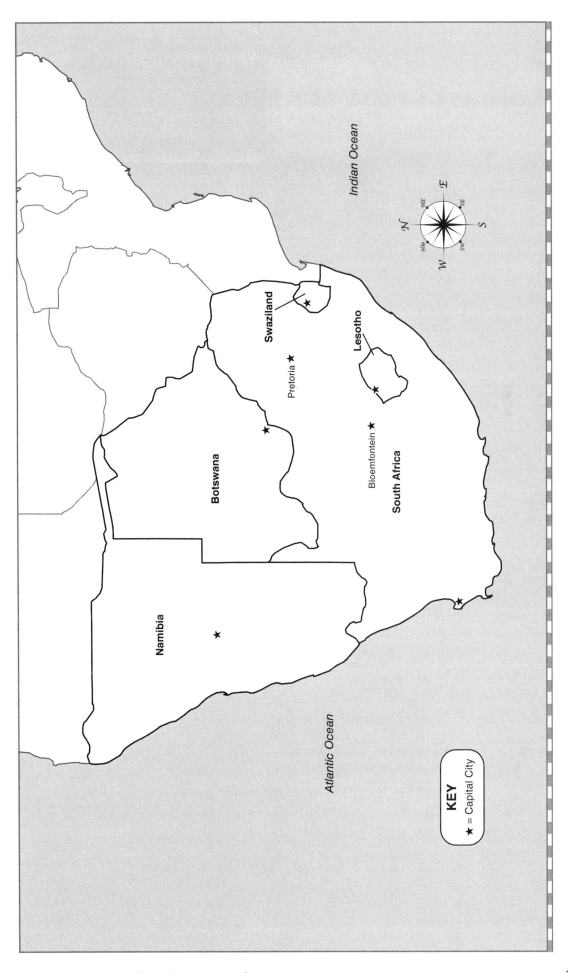

Indian Ocean

Swaziland

Lesotho

Pretoria ★

Bloemfontein ★

South Africa

Botswana

Namibia

Atlantic Ocean

KEY
★ = Capital City

Largest Cities of Africa

	City	Country	Population
1	Lagos	Nigeria	8,029,200
2	Cairo	Egypt	7,764,700
3	Kinshasa	Dem. Rep. of the Congo	6,301,100
4	Alexandria	Egypt	3,806,300
5	Casablanca	Morocco	3,344,300
6	Abidjan	Côte d'Ivoire	3,310,500
7	Kano	Nigeria	3,248,700
8	Ibadan	Nigeria	3,078,400
9	Cape Town	South Africa	2,686,000
10	Addis Ababa	Ethiopia	2,638,500
11	Giza	Egypt	2,541,000
12	Nairobi	Kenya	2,510,800
13	Dar es Salaam	Tanzania	2,456,100
14	Dakar	Senegal	2,384,000
15	Durban	South Africa	2,354,900
16	Luanda	Angola	2,193,400

Populations are estimates based on figures from official government
and United Nations sources.

Largest Cities of Africa

A. Use the chart on the other page to help you circle the correct answer to each question.

1. Which city has the larger population?   **Cairo**   **Lagos**

2. What is the difference in population between Lagos and Cairo?   **more than 500,000**   **less than 500,000**

3. In which country is Nairobi located?   **Kenya**   **Nigeria**

4. Which city is one of the top 10 most populated?   **Dakar**   **Kano**

5. How many of the most populated cities are located in Nigeria?   **three**   **four**

6. Which city has a population of about 2.2 million?   **Luanda**   **Durban**

7. What is the difference in population between the largest and 16th-largest cities?   **under 5 million**   **over 5 million**

8. In which country is Dakar located?   **South Africa**   **Senegal**

9. How many of the most populated cities are located in Egypt?   **three**   **four**

10. Which city has a population of 2,686,000?   **Cape Town**   **Ibadan**

11. The 13th-largest city is located in which country?   **Morocco**   **Tanzania**

B. New York City is the most populated city in the United States, with about 8,364,000 people. If New York City were located in Africa, what would its ranking be among the largest cities?

_____

Review

Use words from the box to complete the crossword puzzle.

billion
country
Eastern
island
Lagos
Nigeria
second
Sudan

Across

2. Africa is the _____-largest continent.

7. _____ is the third-largest country in size.

8. _____ is the most populated country.

Down

1. Africa has about one _____ people.

3. _____ Africa has the largest number of countries.

4. The Seychelles are the smallest island _____.

5. Madagascar is the largest _____ nation in Africa.

6. _____ is the largest city in Africa.

Physical Features of Africa

This section introduces students to the landforms and bodies of water of Africa. Students discover that Africa has high mountains, dry deserts, vast plains, and tropical islands. They also find out that it has the world's longest river and many amazing waterfalls. Students become familiar with the major oceans, seas, gulfs, and waterways that surround Africa.

Each skill in this section is based on the following National Geography Standards:

Essential Element 2: Places and Regions

Standard 4: The physical and human characteristics of places

Essential Element 3: Physical Systems

Standards 7 & 8: The physical processes that shape the patterns of Earth's surface, and the characteristics and spatial distribution of ecosystems on Earth's surface

CONTENTS

Overview

The equator runs through the middle of Africa. This means that about 90% of the continent lies within the tropics, giving most of Africa a warm or hot climate. The amount of rainfall varies greatly from region to region, resulting in diverse landscapes—from arid deserts to lush rainforests.

Landforms

Africa has a wide variety of landforms. The continent is covered by deserts, grasslands, forests, and mountains.

Africa has three major deserts. The Sahara Desert in the northern part of the continent is one of the largest deserts in the world. The other two deserts are the Kalahari and Namib deserts in the south.

Grasslands and forests cover the majority of the continent. Grasslands called *savannas* extend from the Atlantic coast to Eastern Africa and from south of the Sahara almost to the southern tip of the continent. Most of the forests in Africa are tropical rainforests, which are mainly found in the Congo Basin.

Volcanic activity created most of the continent's highest mountains. The two tallest peaks are Mount Kilimanjaro in Tanzania and Mount Kenya in Kenya. Volcanic activity also produced the Ethiopian Highlands in Eastern Africa. The Atlas Mountains, a nonvolcanic range found in northwest Africa, is the longest mountain system on the continent.

Bodies of Water

Water surrounds the continent of Africa on nearly all sides. The 80-mile (130-km) wide Sinai Peninsula in Egypt connects Africa and Asia. If it weren't for this narrow stretch of land, Africa would be a gigantic island!

Two oceans and two seas border Africa. The continent sits between the Atlantic Ocean to the west and south and the Indian Ocean to the east. The Mediterranean and the Red seas border the northeast coast of Africa. The Strait of Gibraltar, a narrow strip of water that connects the Mediterranean Sea and the Atlantic Ocean, separates Africa from Europe.

Africa has the longest river in the world—the Nile. The continent also has three other major rivers—the Congo, the Niger, and the Zambezi. A world-famous waterfall called Victoria Falls is located on the Zambezi River. Most of Africa's large lakes, including Lake Victoria and Lake Tanganyika, lie in the eastern part of the continent.

Overview

Fill in the bubble to answer each question or complete each sentence.

1. The _____ runs through the middle of the continent, giving Africa a warm climate.
   - Ⓐ desert
   - Ⓑ equator
   - Ⓒ rainforest
   - Ⓓ savanna

2. The longest mountain system in Africa is _____.
   - Ⓐ Mt. Kilimanjaro
   - Ⓑ Mt. Kenya
   - Ⓒ the Atlas Mountains
   - Ⓓ the Ethiopian Highlands

3. What kind of landform is the Sahara?
   - Ⓐ desert
   - Ⓑ savanna
   - Ⓒ mountain
   - Ⓓ rainforest

4. Which statement is true about Africa?
   - Ⓐ No oceans border Africa.
   - Ⓑ The Atlantic and Indian oceans border Africa.
   - Ⓒ The Atlantic and Pacific oceans border Africa.
   - Ⓓ All four oceans border the continent of Africa.

5. The _____ is the longest river in the world.
   - Ⓐ Congo River
   - Ⓑ Niger River
   - Ⓒ Zambezi River
   - Ⓓ Nile River

Name _____

Africa's Natural Landscape

Africa is an immense plateau, which means that the entire continent is a high plain with fairly flat terrain. Hot, dry deserts cover two-fifths of Africa. Savannas also cover more than two-fifths of the continent. Rainforests make up the last fifth and are found in the Congo Basin, parts of Western Africa, and Madagascar. There are mountains in Africa as well. The Atlas Mountains in the north and the Ethiopian Highlands in the east are major mountain regions.

A. Use the information above and the map on the other page to answer the questions.

1. Which desert is the largest in Africa?   _____

2. What is the name of the major peak shown on the map?   _____

3. Where is the Horn of Africa located, on the eastern side   _____
   of Africa or the western side?

4. Which mountains are located in Northern Africa?   _____

5. The Congo Basin is a rainforest area. In what part of   _____
   Africa—north, south, or central—is it located?

6. How much of Africa is covered by savannas?   _____

7. Is the Great Rift Valley located on the eastern or   _____
   western side of the continent?

8. On which island are there rainforests?   _____

B. Circle the names of the landforms labeled on the map. Use the colors listed below for each landform.

> **Deserts:** yellow   **Horn of Africa:** red
>
> **Congo Basin:** green   **Mountains and**
>   **Highlands:** brown
> **Great Rift Valley:** orange

Africa's Natural Landscape

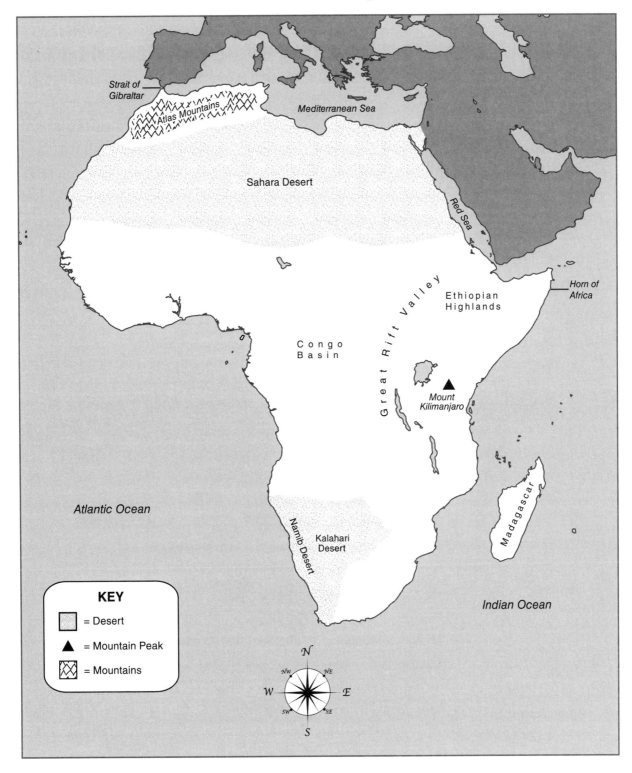

Strait of Gibraltar

Atlas Mountains

Mediterranean Sea

Sahara Desert

Red Sea

Horn of Africa

Great Rift Valley

Ethiopian Highlands

Congo Basin

Mount Kilimanjaro

Atlantic Ocean

Namib Desert

Kalahari Desert

Madagascar

Indian Ocean

KEY

▢ = Desert

▲ = Mountain Peak

▨ = Mountains

N
NW   NE
W   E
SW   SE
S

Mount Kilimanjaro

Fast Facts

- Kilimanjaro is called the "roof of Africa" because it is the highest point in Africa.

- Kilimanjaro is the tallest freestanding (meaning not part of a range) mountain in the world.

- Kilimanjaro is also known as the "White Mountain." Even though it is near the equator, the mountain is ice-capped. However, scientists say the glaciers on the mountain are melting at an alarmingly fast rate.

- The mountain is 19,340 feet (5,895 m) high. It measures 25 miles (40 km) across at its widest part.

- Kilimanjaro is an inactive *stratovolcano*. A stratovolcano is a tall, conical volcano that can have explosive eruptions.

- Kilimanjaro has three main volcanic cones—Kibo, Mawenzi, and Shira—and a number of smaller cones. Of the three main cones, only Kibo is a *dormant* volcano. It is inactive, but expected to become active again. The last time it erupted was 200 years ago. Mawenzi and Shira are *extinct* volcanoes, meaning they will never erupt again.

- About 22,000 people climb Kilimanjaro each year. About 40% of these climbers turn back before they reach the summit.

There are six different ecological zones, or areas with distinct habitats, on Mount Kilimanjaro. They are:

Zone	Elevation	Interesting Facts
Bushland (farmland and wild grasses)	2,600 to 6,000 feet (800 to 1,800 m)	Coffee is grown at this level.
Rainforest	6,000 to 9,200 feet (1,800 to 2,800 m)	About 72 inches (183 cm) of rain falls here annually.
Heath	9,200 to 11,000 feet (2,800 to 3,350 m)	Heather plants, which are usually small, can grow up to 33 feet (10 m) tall here.
Moorland	11,000 to 13,200 feet (3,350 to 4,000 m)	Large birds of prey such as the crowned eagle are often seen here.
Alpine Desert	13,200 to 16,500 feet (4,000 to 5,000 m)	Temperatures can vary from 100°F (38°C) during the day to below freezing at night.
Summit	16,500 to 19,340 feet (5,000 to 5,895 m)	Slow-growing lichens, perhaps among the oldest living things on Earth, grow at the summit.

Mount Kilimanjaro

A. Read each statement. Circle **yes** if it is true or **no** if it is false. Use the information on the other page to help you.

1. Kilimanjaro is the tallest mountain in Africa.   **Yes**   **No**

2. Kilimanjaro is a freestanding mountain.   **Yes**   **No**

3. The mountain is more than 20,000 feet (6,096 m) high.   **Yes**   **No**

4. Even though Kilimanjaro is near the equator, it is ice-capped.   **Yes**   **No**

5. Kilimanjaro is an active stratovolcano.   **Yes**   **No**

6. Kibo is the only volcanic cone on Kilimanjaro.   **Yes**   **No**

7. Everyone who climbs Kilimanjaro reaches the summit.   **Yes**   **No**

8. There are six ecological zones on the mountain.   **Yes**   **No**

9. A climber in the heath zone of the mountain will see tall heather plants growing there.   **Yes**   **No**

10. Coffee is grown in the rainforest zone of the mountain.   **Yes**   **No**

B. Color and label each of the six ecological zones of Mount Kilimanjaro.

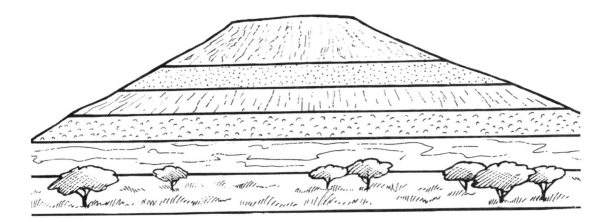

Great Rift Valley

The Great Rift Valley is actually a series of valleys that run through much of Eastern Africa. The Great Rift Valley is about 4,000 miles (6,400 km) long. Most parts of the valley are from 18 to 60 miles (30 to 100 km) wide, with steep walls that rise about 6,600 feet (2,000 m) high in some places.

The formation of the Great Rift Valley can be explained by the theory of *plate tectonics*. This theory states that Earth's hard outer shell, or crust, is divided into large sections called *plates*. The plates move very slowly over the surface of Earth. As the plates move, they come together, move apart, or slide past each other. The continents lie on the plates and move along with them. Eastern Africa lies on the African Plate. About 20 million years ago, the plate began to split apart, causing an immense *fault,* or crack, to form.

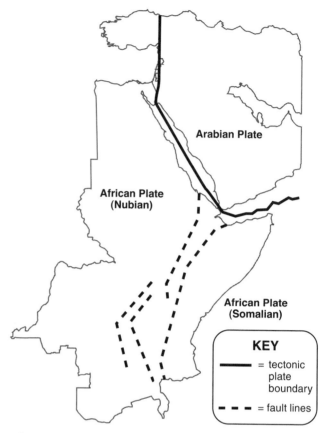

The African Plate is splitting into the Nubian and Somalian plates along different fault lines in Eastern Africa.

Today, the Great Rift Valley is the longest fault system in the world. It has some of Africa's most beautiful scenery, including sparkling, pink-colored lakes. These lakes, called soda lakes, have high concentrations of a type of salt that makes them appear pink in color. However, the water in the lakes is poisonous to most animals.

There are also active, dormant, and extinct volcanoes in the Great Rift Valley. In the past 150 years, more than 110 volcanic eruptions have been reported in 18 locations. Scientists have identified another 112 volcanoes that are dormant.

Scientists think that if the plates in this area of Africa continue to move apart, Eastern Africa will split from the continent and form a new landmass. But this won't happen for millions of years.

Great Rift Valley

Use the information on the other page to answer the questions below.

1. What are two physical features of the Great Rift Valley?

   _____

2. What makes some lakes in the Great Rift Valley appear pink in color?

   _____

3. Name three ways that tectonic plates move.

   _____

   _____

4. How many dormant volcanoes are there in the Great Rift Valley?

   _____

5. What two plates is the African Plate splitting into?

   _____

6. How was the Great Rift Valley formed?

   _____

   _____

7. What do scientists believe will eventually happen to Eastern Africa?

   _____

   _____

Africa's Deserts

Africa has three major deserts—the Sahara, the Kalahari, and the Namib.

Sahara Desert

Namib Desert

Kalahari Desert

Sahara Desert

The Sahara is the largest desert in Africa. It is also the largest hot desert in the world. (Some deserts can be cool or even frozen). Located in Northern Africa, the Sahara covers about 3½ million square miles (9 million square km), which is about the size of the United States. The desert runs through 10 countries and one territory (Western Sahara).

The Sahara has huge seas of sand, called *ergs,* that form sand dunes as high as 600 feet (180 m). But the desert is more than just sand. The Sahara also has mountains, rocky areas, gravel plains, and salt flats. The climate is hot and dry, with an average yearly rainfall of less than 4 inches (10 cm). Summer temperatures average above 90°F (32°C). The highest recorded temperature in the Sahara is 136°F (58°C). Winter temperatures average from 50°F to 60°F (10°C to 16°C).

Kalahari Desert

The Kalahari covers an area of about 190,000 square miles (500,000 square km) in southwestern Africa. It makes up much of the country of Botswana, as well as parts of Namibia and South Africa.

Some scientists do not consider the Kalahari a true desert. A true desert is *arid,* meaning there is very little rainfall. True deserts receive less than 10 inches (25 cm) of rain a year. The northeastern part of the Kalahari is *semiarid,* receiving up to 20 inches (50 cm) annually. Temperatures are rather mild, ranging from 86°F (30°C) in the summer to 40°F (4.4°C) in the winter. Drought-resistant grasses are found in this part of the Kalahari.

The arid southeastern part of the Kalahari gets only about 8 inches (20 cm) of rain a year. Temperatures there can reach more than 100°F (38°C). Red sands and dunes cover large areas in the southeastern Kalahari.

Namib Desert

The Namib Desert lies along Africa's southwestern coast in Namibia. It has an area of about 31,200 square miles (80,800 square km). Large expanses of sand stretch along the coast. These coastal sands form some of the highest dunes in the world, reaching as high as 1,300 feet (400 m). Farther inland, the land is rocky. The Namib Desert has a harsh climate. Wind, fog, and mist are common, so the desert is mostly cool. Little rain falls in this area. The coastal desert receives less than ¾ inch (2 cm) of rain a year.

Africa's Deserts

A. Read each statement and circle the desert that is described. Use the information on the other page to help you.

1.	This desert is the largest in Africa.	**Kalahari**	**Sahara**
2.	Some scientists do not think this is a true desert because it receives too much rain.	**Kalahari**	**Namib**
3.	This desert has some of the highest sand dunes in the world.	**Sahara**	**Namib**
4.	This desert is about the size of the United States.	**Namib**	**Sahara**
5.	This desert lies along Africa's southwestern coast.	**Namib**	**Kalahari**
6.	With an area of about 190,000 squares miles, this desert is the second largest in Africa.	**Kalahari**	**Namib**
7.	This desert's highest recorded temperature is 136°F (58°C).	**Kalahari**	**Sahara**
8.	Wind, fog, and mist are common in this desert.	**Namib**	**Kalahari**
9.	This desert has seas of sand called ergs.	**Sahara**	**Namib**
10.	Much of Botswana and parts of Namibia and South Africa are covered by this desert.	**Sahara**	**Kalahari**

B. Which of the three deserts—Sahara, Kalahari, or Namib—do you think could support plants and animals the best? Explain your answer.

_____

_____

_____

African Savanna

A savanna is a large area of wide-open grassland with a few scattered trees and shrubs. This type of land covers 28 countries in Africa—almost half of the continent.

The savanna has two seasons—dry and wet. The dry season lasts over seven months. The average temperatures during the dry season range from 81°F to 86°F (27°C to 30°C). During the rainy season, the savanna receives between 20 and 60 inches (50 and 150 cm) of rain.

Tall grasses, thorny bushes, and short trees grow in the savanna. The grasses can reach 10 feet (3 m) high during the rainy season. They grow in tufts around sections of bare ground. During the dry season, the tufts die, leaving only roots.

The umbrella-shaped *acacia tree* is the most common tree in the savanna. During the rainy season, acacia trees create leafy canopies that are flattened by winds. In the dry season, the trees lose their leaves to conserve moisture. Another tree called the *baobab* stores water in its trunk. Its thick bark protects it from fires in the dry season.

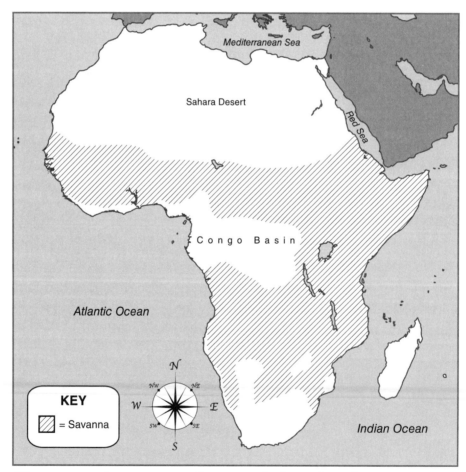

The savanna forms a curve that extends from the Atlantic coast south of the Sahara Desert, across to Eastern Africa, and then back westward to the Atlantic coast south of the Congo Basin.

African Savanna

A. Complete each sentence by unscrambling the word under the line. Use the information on the other page to help you.

1. African grasslands are called _____.
   annavass

2. There are only two _____ in the African savanna.
   soesnas

3. Grasslands cover almost half of the _____.
   centinotn

4. The savanna stretches across 28 _____ in Africa.
   csoeuinrt

5. The savanna is made up mostly of tall _____, thorny
   bushes, and small trees.   **sregsas**

6. The _____ tree stores water in its trunk.
   obbaab

7. _____ trees are the most common trees on the savanna.
   aaccai

8. During the dry season, average _____ are from 81°F to 86°F.
   mutespretare

B. Write four more facts you learned about the African savanna, its seasons, or the plants that grow there.

1. _____

2. _____

3. _____

4. _____

Africa's Rainforests

Africa has three areas of rainforest. The largest is called the Congo Basin Rainforest. There are also rainforests in Western Africa and on the island of Madagascar. Altogether, these rainforests cover about one-fifth of the continent. They are home to half of all the animal species of Africa.

Congo Basin Rainforest

The Congo Basin Rainforest is the second-largest rainforest in the world. Only the Amazon Rainforest in South America is larger. The Congo Basin Rainforest covers about 540,000 square miles (1.4 million square km) of land, an area about twice the size of France. The rainforest runs through the countries of Cameroon, the Central African Republic, the Democratic Republic of the Congo, Equatorial Guinea, Gabon, and Republic of the Congo.

In the Congo Basin Rainforest, there are more than 600 different species of trees and 10,000 animal species. The rainforest is known for its mountain gorillas and forest elephants.

The Congo Basin Rainforest is one of the world's most threatened natural habitats. Widespread *deforestation*—or clearing of the land—has occurred because of logging, farming, and wars.

Elephants roam the Congo Basin.

Western Africa's Rainforests

Western Africa's rainforests are also disappearing. In the past 15 years, about 26% of the forest has been cut down or destroyed. The rainforest is home to many of Africa's mammals, including lowland gorillas and chimpanzees. There are about 1,800 species of plants.

Chimpanzees graze in Western Africa's rainforest.

Rainforests of Madagascar

Madagascar has rainforests in the eastern part of the island. Like the other two rainforest areas of Africa, Madagascar's rainforests are in danger. Scientists estimate that Madagascar has about 250,000 species of plants and animals that exist nowhere else on Earth. For example, lemurs can only be found in Madagascar.

Lemurs live only in the rainforest of Madagascar.

Africa's Rainforests

Write the names of the three numbered rainforest areas on the map key. Then color the rainforest areas three different colors. Complete the map key by writing the color you used for each rainforest.

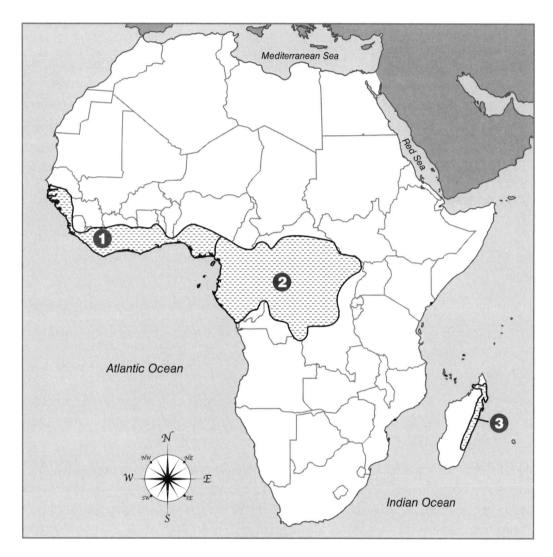

MAP KEY

Rainforest Name   **Color**

1. _____   _____

2. _____   _____

3. _____   _____

Madagascar

The continent of Africa includes many islands and island countries that lie in the Atlantic and Indian oceans. The largest island nation is Madagascar. Its official name is the Republic of Madagascar. The country consists of one large island, also called Madagascar, and tiny nearby islands.

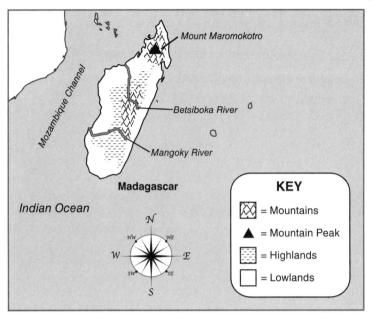

The island of Madagascar, about the size of New York State, is the largest island in Africa and the fourth largest in the world. About 160 million years ago, the island split off from the mainland. Now, the Mozambique Channel in the Indian Ocean separates Madagascar from mainland Africa, which is about 240 miles (386 km) to the west.

Madagascar has five main regions that include a variety of landforms and climates.

Northern Region: Northern Madagascar is mountainous. The mountains cut off northern Madagascar from the rest of the island. Mount Maromokotro, located in this region, is the highest mountain on the island at 9,436 feet (2,876 m).

Western Region: Western Madagascar has wide plains and some fertile river valleys. This region is home to dry, *deciduous* forests, or forests with trees that lose their leaves during the fall.

Eastern Region: A narrow plain lies along the east coast. Here, tropical storms called cyclones are common during the months of February and March. Rainforests used to flourish in the area, but now they are smaller. Most that remain are national parks so they can be protected.

Central Region: Central Madagascar consists of highlands that are at elevations of 2,000 to 4,000 feet (610 to 1,200 m), as well as some higher mountains. The area is known for its red soil created by the weathering of iron-rich rock.

Southern Region: The southern part of Madagascar has a hot, dry climate that receives little rainfall. Scientists can't agree on whether to call the area a forest or a desert, so they call it a *thicket*. Because the trees often have long, sharp spines, the area is known as the Spiny Thicket.

Madagascar

Read each clue below. Write the correct word on the numbered lines. Then use the numbers to crack the code!

1. Madagascar is the _____ island in Africa.

   $\overline{9}$ $\overline{17}$ $\overline{5}$ $\overline{12}$ $\overline{14}$ $\overline{4}$ $\overline{3}$

2. _____ Maromokotro is the highest mountain on the island.

   $\overline{8}$ $\overline{6}$ $\overline{2}$ $\overline{7}$ $\overline{3}$

3. Tropical storms called _____ cause destruction on Madagascar.

   $\overline{16}$ $\overline{1}$ $\overline{16}$ $\overline{9}$ $\overline{6}$ $\overline{7}$ $\overline{14}$ $\overline{4}$

4. Tropical _____ are found in the eastern regions of Madagascar.

   $\overline{5}$ $\overline{17}$ $\overline{10}$ $\overline{7}$ $\overline{13}$ $\overline{6}$ $\overline{5}$ $\overline{14}$ $\overline{4}$ $\overline{3}$ $\overline{4}$

5. Central Madagascar has many _____, as well as some taller mountains.

   $\overline{11}$ $\overline{10}$ $\overline{12}$ $\overline{11}$ $\overline{9}$ $\overline{17}$ $\overline{7}$ $\overline{15}$ $\overline{4}$

6. The Spiny Thicket is similar to both a _____ and a forest.

   $\overline{15}$ $\overline{14}$ $\overline{4}$ $\overline{14}$ $\overline{5}$ $\overline{3}$

Crack the Code!

Madagascar's nickname is the _____.

$\overline{12}$ $\overline{5}$ $\overline{14}$ $\overline{17}$ $\overline{3}$ $\overline{5}$ $\overline{14}$ $\overline{15}$ $\overline{10}$ $\overline{4}$ $\overline{9}$ $\overline{17}$ $\overline{7}$ $\overline{15}$

Africa's Bodies of Water

The Atlantic and Indian oceans border Africa to the west and east. Two major seas—the Mediterranean Sea and the Red Sea—border the continent to the north. The Gulf of Guinea, which is part of the Atlantic Ocean, and the Gulf of Aden, which is part of the Indian Ocean, also form some of the coastline of the continent.

Other bodies of water help separate mainland Africa from nearby landmasses. The narrow Strait of Gibraltar separates Africa from the European country of Spain. The Mozambique Channel divides the large island of Madagascar from the rest of the continent.

Within the continent, there are many rivers and lakes. The four longest rivers are the Nile, Congo, Niger, and Zambezi. The largest lake is Lake Victoria. Lake Tanganyika and Lake Nyasa are also large lakes located in Eastern Africa.

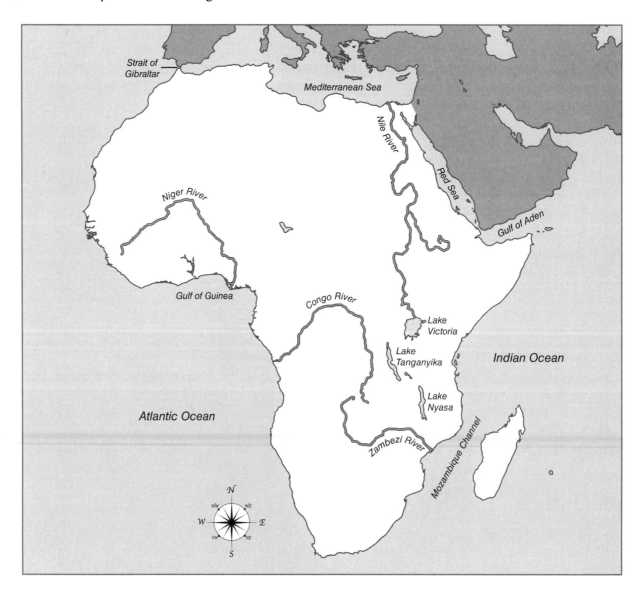

Africa's Bodies of Water

A. Find and circle the lakes, rivers, seas, and oceans in the word puzzle.
Words may appear across, down, or diagonally.

```
M  D  J  U  H  D  W  A  T  L  A  N  T  I  C
E  E  G  J  O  N  S  A  R  B  O  Q  A  C  H
D  F  N  R  V  Y  A  E  B  C  W  P  X  R  A
I  G  T  N  Y  A  S  A  K  A  B  C  D  Z  A
T  V  T  A  N  G  A  N  Y  I  K  A  A  T  R
E  B  C  E  A  E  P  Q  S  A  B  M  D  A  Z
R  E  Y  R  L  J  Q  N  A  E  B  N  U  K  A
R  C  A  I  B  R  C  I  P  E  C  I  D  O  M
A  U  N  T  E  I  R  U  Z  E  G  N  R  C  B
N  E  I  G  L  O  C  I  S  A  J  D  S  K  E
E  F  I  M  T  G  I  W  J  B  H  I  Q  U  Z
A  N  D  C  R  H  E  C  K  D  T  A  T  O  I
N  R  I  D  C  O  N  G  O  C  R  N  O  I  J
T  V  O  W  A  E  D  I  S  L  S  E  W  N  U
U  I  P  K  B  T  J  N  A  R  F  I  D  S  K
```

Oceans:
  Atlantic
  Indian

Seas:
  Mediterranean
  Red

Rivers:
  Congo
  Nile
  Zambezi

Lakes:
  Nyasa
  Tanganyika
  Victoria

B. Write three facts you learned about Africa's bodies of water. Use the information
and map on the other page to help you.

1. _____

_____

2. _____

_____

3. _____

_____

Name _____

Africa's Lakes

There are many lakes in the Rift Valley of Eastern Africa. The three largest lakes are Lake Victoria, Lake Tanganyika, and Lake Nyasa (also called Lake Malawi).

Africa's Rift Valley

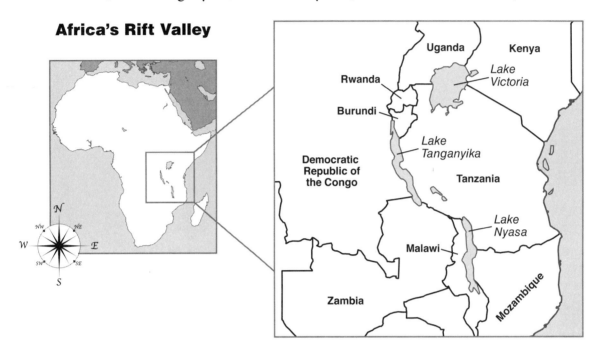

Name	Size (Approximate)	Interesting Facts
Lake Victoria	*Area:* 26,800 square miles (69,500 square km) *Depth:* 276 feet (84 m)	• largest freshwater lake in Africa; second largest in the world • located in three countries: Kenya, Tanzania, and Uganda • has many small islands
Lake Tanganyika	*Area:* 12,700 square miles (32,900 square km) *Depth:* 4,820 feet (1,470 m)	• measures 420 miles (680 km) from end to end; longest freshwater lake in Africa and in the world • located in four countries: Burundi, Democratic Republic of the Congo, Tanzania, and Zambia • deepest lake in Africa; second deepest in the world • crocodiles and hippos live on its shores
Lake Nyasa (Lake Malawi)	*Area:* 11,430 square miles (29,600 square km) *Depth:* 2,300 feet (701 m)	• third-largest lake in Africa; tenth largest in the world • located in three countries: Malawi, Mozambique, and Tanzania • has clear water to a depth of 70 feet (21 m) • has more fish species than any other lake in the world

Africa's Lakes

Read each statement and circle the lake that is described. Use the information and map on the other page to help you.

1. This lake is the largest freshwater lake in Africa.   **Victoria**   **Nyasa**

2. This lake has clear water to a depth of 70 feet.   **Nyasa**   **Tanganyika**

3. This lake is located in the countries of Malawi, Mozambique, and Tanzania.   **Victoria**   **Nyasa**

4. This lake measures 420 miles from end to end.   **Victoria**   **Tanganyika**

5. This lake is also known as Lake Malawi.   **Nyasa**   **Tanganyika**

6. The countries of Kenya, Tanzania, and Uganda share this lake.   **Victoria**   **Nyasa**

7. This lake is the deepest lake in Africa and the second deepest in the world.   **Victoria**   **Tanganyika**

8. This lake has an area of 26,800 square miles (69,500 square km).   **Nyasa**   **Victoria**

9. This lake has more fish species than any other lake in the world.   **Nyasa**   **Victoria**

10. Crocodiles and hippos are found on the shores of this lake.   **Victoria**   **Tanganyika**

11. This lake has a depth of 2,300 feet.   **Victoria**   **Nyasa**

12. This lake has many small islands.   **Nyasa**   **Victoria**

13. This lake is located farthest south in Africa.   **Victoria**   **Nyasa**

14. This lake is located east of Rwanda.   **Victoria**   **Tanganyika**

Major Rivers of Africa

When geographers talk about rivers, they use the following terms to describe sections of the river:

Source—This is where the river begins. It may be a lake, a stream, an underground spring, or another river.

Course—This is the route the river follows. Other rivers, called *tributaries,* may join the main river along the way.

Mouth—This is where the river ends, flowing into a larger body of water. Sometimes the mouth of the river creates a *delta,* or a fan-shaped area of land, formed from mud and sand that has been deposited by the river.

The chart below shows the characteristics of the major rivers of Africa.

River	Length	Source	Course	Mouth
Nile	4,160 miles (6,695 km) longest in Africa and in the world	Lake Victoria	flows north through 11 countries in northeast Africa, making a snake-like shape	empties into the Nile Delta and then into the Mediterranean Sea
Congo	2,900 miles (4,667 km) second longest in Africa and fifth longest in the world	the place where the Lualaba and Luvua rivers meet in the southern part of the Democratic Republic of the Congo	flows north and turns southwest through 8 countries in west-central Africa, making a C shape	empties into the South Atlantic Ocean
Niger	2,600 miles (4,184 km) third longest in Africa	the highlands of southern Guinea	flows northeast and then turns southeast through 5 countries in Western Africa	empties into the Niger Delta and then into the Gulf of Guinea
Zambezi	1,700 miles (2,735 km) fourth longest in Africa	the wetlands of northwestern Zambia	flows south and then turns southeast through 6 countries in southeast Africa, making an S shape	empties into the Zambezi Delta and then into the Mozambique Channel

Major Rivers of Africa

A. Fill in the blanks with the correct names of the major rivers of Africa. Use the information on the other page to help you.

1. The _____ River is the longest river in Africa.

2. The _____ River flows through six countries in southeast Africa, making an S shape.

3. The _____ River is 2,600 miles long.

4. The _____ River flows through eight countries in west-central Africa.

5. The _____ River is the third-longest river in Africa.

6. The _____ River is 4,160 miles long.

7. The _____ River is the fifth longest in the world.

8. The _____ River empties into the Zambezi Delta.

B. Draw a line to match each source to its river. Then draw a line to match the river to its mouth.

Source	River	Mouth
Southern Guinea •	• **Nile** •	• South Atlantic Ocean
Lake Victoria •	• **Congo** •	• Gulf of Guinea
Northwest Zambia •	• **Niger** •	• Mediterranean Sea
Lualaba and Luvua Rivers •	• **Zambezi** •	• Mozambique Channel

Amazing Waterfalls of Africa

A waterfall is a river or stream that flows over the edge of a cliff. There are 45 major waterfalls in Africa. The highest and widest ones are Tugela Falls and Victoria Falls.

Tugela Falls

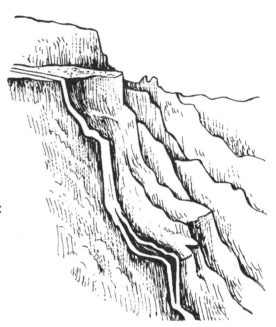

- located in a national park in South Africa
- source: Tugela River
- highest waterfall in Africa and second highest in the world
- height: 3,110 feet (948 m)
- width: 50 feet (15 m)
- average volume of water spilled each second: 50 cubic feet (1 cubic m)
- five separate *tiers,* or drops
- longest single tier is 1,350 feet (411 m)

Victoria Falls

- located in a national park on the border between Zambia and Zimbabwe
- source: Zambezi River
- widest waterfall in Africa and in the world
- height: 350 feet (107 m)
- width: 5,700 feet (1,737 m)
- average volume of water spilled each second: 38,430 cubic feet (1,088 cubic m)
- falls are composed of four major streams— The Devil's Cataract, Main Falls, Rainbow Falls, and the Eastern Cataract

Name _____

Amazing Waterfalls of Africa

A. Read each statement. Circle **yes** if it is true or **no** if it is false. Use the information on the other page to help you.

1. Victoria Falls is the widest waterfall in Africa.   Yes   No

2. Tugela Falls is the highest waterfall in the world.   Yes   No

3. The water source for Victoria Falls is the Zambezi River.   Yes   No

4. Both Tugela Falls and Victoria Falls are located in national parks.   Yes   No

5. Tugela Falls is 50 feet high and 3,110 feet wide.   Yes   No

6. There are five separate tiers of Tugela Falls.   Yes   No

7. Victoria Falls is located on the border of Zambia and Zimbabwe.   Yes   No

8. One section of Victoria Falls is called the Devil's Cataract.   Yes   No

9. A higher volume of water spills over Tugela Falls than
   Victoria Falls.   Yes   No

10. The longest single drop of Tugela Falls is 1,350 feet (411 m).   Yes   No

B. Use the information on the other page to label Tugela Falls and Victoria Falls on the map below.

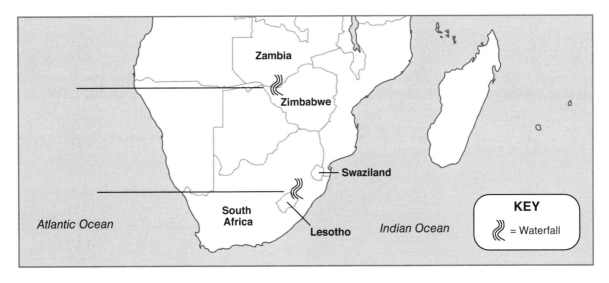

Review

Use words from the box to complete the crossword puzzle.

Congo

Kilimanjaro

Nile

Sahara

savanna

Tugela

Victoria

Across

5. _____ Falls is the highest waterfall in Africa.

6. the largest desert in Africa

7. the longest river in Africa and the world

Down

1. Lake _____ is the largest in Africa.

2. The _____ Basin is the second-largest rainforest in the world.

3. The highest mountain on the continent is _____.

4. another name for African grasslands

Valuable Resources of Africa

This section introduces students to the natural resources of Africa. Students learn the top 10 oil-producing countries and discover that gold and diamonds are mined in Africa. Students also learn about farming practices and find out that cacao and coffee are two important African crops. Students discover the importance of the Nile River as a water source for a number of countries. Finally, students learn about some of the many interesting and unusual animals of Africa.

Each skill in this section is based on the following National Geography Standards:

Essential Element 3: Physical Systems

> **Standard 8:** The characteristics and spatial distribution of ecosystems on Earth's surface

Essential Element 5: Environment and Society

> **Standard 14:** How human actions modify the physical environment

> **Standard 16:** The changes that occur in the meaning, use, distribution, and importance of resources

CONTENTS

Overview

Natural resources are the oil, gas, minerals, water, soil, plants, and other elements that people use from their environment. The animals that make their home on a continent are also valuable resources. Africa has all these valuable resources and more.

Oil and Minerals

Oil is an important natural resource in Africa. Nigeria, Algeria, and Angola are the top three producers of oil. Countries along the Gulf of Guinea are increasing their production of oil through offshore and deep-sea drilling.

Africa is also rich in valuable minerals, such as gold and diamonds. South Africa and Ghana mine the most gold in Africa. Bostwana and the Democratic Republic of the Congo are the top diamond producers.

Organic and Traditional Farming

About two-thirds of all Africans live in rural areas where they make a living growing crops and raising livestock. Most farmers have small parcels of land on which they grow *staple crops*—crops that are basic to the people's diet, such as corn, wheat, and millet. Many African farmers are switching to organic farming. They use all-natural farming practices that keep the soil rich in nutrients.

Larger African farms produce crops that are exported to other countries. Two popular crops are *cacao* (kuh-COW), from which chocolate is made, and coffee. The country of Côte d'Ivoire is the top producer of cacao in the world. Ethiopia is the top producer of coffee in Africa.

Sharing the Nile

Water is a vital natural resource. The Nile River is the longest river in the world, and about 300 million people depend on it for water. Eleven countries in the Nile River Basin share the waters of the Nile. Egypt and Sudan take the largest share. The other countries are working with Egypt and Sudan to make a fair agreement for sharing.

Africa's Amazing Wild Animals

Africa has many unique wild animals. On the savanna, over 2 million wildebeest, zebras, and antelope migrate every year across the Serengeti Plains of Tanzania looking for fresh grass and water. Fennec foxes, meerkats, and sidewinder snakes survive in the hot and barren deserts of Africa. And the rainforests of Africa are home to the endangered mandrill, lowland gorilla, and ruffed lemur. Thousands of tourists flock to the continent to see these animals in their natural habitats. They go on safaris hoping to see the "big five"—Cape buffalo, elephant, leopard, lion, and rhinoceros.

Overview

Fill in the bubble to answer each question or complete each sentence.

1. Which country is *not* a top producer of oil?

   Ⓐ Algeria

   Ⓑ Angola

   Ⓒ Nigeria

   Ⓓ South Africa

2. Which country is a top producer of diamonds?

   Ⓐ Angola

   Ⓑ Botswana

   Ⓒ Nigeria

   Ⓓ South Africa

3. Two major crops of Africa that are shipped to other countries are cacao and _____.

   Ⓐ corn

   Ⓑ wheat

   Ⓒ millet

   Ⓓ coffee

4. _____ African countries depend on the Nile River.

   Ⓐ Five

   Ⓑ Eight

   Ⓒ Ten

   Ⓓ Twenty

5. Which animals migrate across the Serengeti Plains every year?

   Ⓐ zebras and wildebeest

   Ⓑ meerkats and gorillas

   Ⓒ antelope and meerkats

   Ⓓ rhinoceroses and foxes

Oil Production in Africa

Oil is a *fossil fuel,* meaning it was formed from the remains of plants and animals that lived millions of years ago. Over time, heat and pressure turned the remains into what is called *crude oil.* Crude oil is a yellowish-black liquid that is usually found in underground reservoirs. A well is drilled into the reservoir to bring the crude oil to the surface. The oil is then sent to a refinery, or factory, where it is made into products such as gasoline and heating oil. Crude oil is often called "black gold" because it is so valuable. It provides much of the world's fuel supply, is expensive to produce, and takes so long to form that there is only a limited supply of it on Earth.

Oil is an important resource in Africa. Three of the top 5 oil-producing countries of Africa border the Mediterranean Sea. They are Algeria, Egypt, and Libya.

Five of the other top oil producers border the Gulf of Guinea. They are Angola, Equatorial Guinea, Gabon, Nigeria, and the Republic of the Congo. Many oil companies are exploring this area of the Atlantic Ocean. Offshore and deep-sea drilling into the bottom of the ocean is increasing along the borders of these five countries.

South Africa is also a large producer and consumer of oil. Even though the country is the 10th-largest producer of oil on the continent, it also has to import oil. It gets oil from other African nations such as Nigeria and Angola to meet its high energy demands.

Africa's Top 10 Oil-Producing Countries in 2010
one barrel = 42 gallons (159 liters)

Rank	Country	Region	Barrels Produced a Day
1	Algeria	Northern Africa	2.18 million
2	Nigeria	Western Africa	2.17 million
3	Angola	Central Africa	2.01 million
4	Libya	Northern Africa	1.88 million
5	Egypt	Northern Africa	631,000
6	Sudan*	Northern Africa	480,000
7	Equatorial Guinea	Central Africa	360,000
8	Republic of the Congo	Central Africa	274,000
9	Gabon	Central Africa	248,000
10	South Africa	Southern Africa	191,000

U.S. Dept. of Energy, Energy Information Administration
*In 2010, Sudan included the country of The Republic of South Sudan.

Oil Production in Africa

A. Read each statement. Circle **yes** if it is true or **no** if it is false. Use the information on the other page to help you.

1. Crude oil is called "black gold" because it's cheap to produce.   **Yes**   **No**

2. Algeria is the top oil producer in Africa.   **Yes**   **No**

3. The top three producers of oil are located in Central Africa.   **Yes**   **No**

4. Four countries produce more than 1 million barrels of oil a day.   **Yes**   **No**

5. The Republic of the Congo and Gabon each produce 274,000 barrels of oil a day.   **Yes**   **No**

6. The Northern African countries of Algeria, Egypt, Libya, and Sudan are among the top five producers of oil in 2010.   **Yes**   **No**

7. Offshore and deep-sea drilling is increasing in the Gulf of Guinea.   **Yes**   **No**

8. In 2010, Sudan ranked right behind Egypt in oil production.   **Yes**   **No**

9. Tenth-ranked South Africa has to import oil from other countries to meet its energy needs.   **Yes**   **No**

10. There is an unlimited supply of oil on Earth.   **Yes**   **No**

B. Nigeria produces about 2,000,000 barrels of oil per day. One barrel equals 42 gallons, or 159 liters. Use this information and your math skills to answer the questions below. Circle the correct answers.

1. About how many gallons of oil does Nigeria produce per day?

   8,400 gallons   **840,000,000 gallons**   **84,000,000 gallons**

2. About how many liters of oil does Nigeria produce per day?

   31,800 liters   **318,000,000 liters**   **3,180,000,000 liters**

3. How does a gallon of oil compare to a liter?

   a gallon is about 4 times larger than a liter   **a liter is about 4 times larger than a gallon**

Mining for Gold and Diamonds

Africa is a major producer of gold. Up to 30% of the world's gold comes from 36 countries in Africa. Mining for gold is difficult, and deposits of pure gold are rare. In nature, gold is usually found within *ore* deposits, or mixtures of metals combined with other minerals. Processing about 10 tons (9 metric tons) of ore yields only about 1 ounce (28 grams) of gold.

Africa is also a major producer of diamonds. About 65% of the world's diamonds come from 18 countries in Africa. Diamonds are also difficult to mine because many tons of rock must be crushed to find one small diamond.

The map and chart below show the top five producers of gold and diamonds in Africa.

Top Five Gold Producers	Top Five Diamond Producers
1. South Africa	1. Botswana
2. Ghana	2. Democratic Republic of the Congo
3. Mali	3. South Africa
4. Tanzania	4. Angola
5. Democratic Republic of the Congo	5. Namibia

Rankings from *U.S. Geological Survey Minerals Yearbook* 2008

Name _____

Mining for Gold and Diamonds

A. Complete each sentence by unscrambling the word under the line. Use the information on the other page to help you.

1. Africa is a major producer of gold and _____.
   dsdnomai

2. _____ is the top producer of diamonds.
   wanabost

3. South Africa is the top producer of _____.
   lgdo

4. The Democratic Republic of the Congo is the fifth-largest producer of gold

   and the _____-largest producer of diamonds.
   sonecd

5. Africa produces about _____ percent of the world's gold.
   hytrit

6. _____ African countries mine diamonds.
   egeniteh

7. The Democratic Republic of the Congo and _____ both
   otuhs acafir
   produce gold and diamonds.

8. About 65% of the world's diamonds come from _____.
   caarif

9. Ten tons of _____ yield only a small amount of gold.
   reo

10. The country of _____ is a top producer of diamonds,
    but not gold.   **baminia**

B. On the map on the other page, color the five gold-producing countries yellow. Color the five diamond-producing countries blue. Two countries will have both colors. In these cases, color each country with yellow and blue stripes.

Farming in Africa

Even though Africa is a continent rich in soil that is easily farmed, many of its people do not have enough food. According to the Food and Agriculture Organization of the United Nations, 265 million people in Africa struggle with hunger daily. That is nearly 30% of Africa's total population. Agricultural experts say that one of the best ways to cut down on hunger is to support *smallholder farmers*—people who own or rent a small farm on which to grow crops and raise animals.

Smallholder Farmers

Eighty percent of farmers in Africa are smallholder farmers. Many of their farms are only about 5 acres. The majority of smallholder farmers are women. They grow the crops to feed their families and to sell at local markets.

The smallholder farmers grow staple crops such as corn, millet, rice, sorghum, and wheat. Other staple crops include peas, peanuts, and beans. Farmers also grow root vegetables such as cassava, potatoes, and yams. Plantains, a member of the banana family, are also grown on these farms. Smallholder farmers produce 80% of the staple foods that are eaten by Africans.

Organic Farming

More and more smallholder farmers are turning to organic farming. They have stopped using chemical fertilizers and pesticides. That saves money, which the farmers can use to buy higher-quality seeds. Also, in the past, farmers burned their fields after harvest. Organic farmers have stopped this practice. Instead, they leave the old plants to rot, which enriches the soil. And the farmers are now rotating their crops so a variety of plants can be planted in the same field.

Hope for the Future

A recent study by the United Nations looked at 114 organic farming projects in 24 African countries. The researchers found that where organic practices had been used, the total amount of crops had more than doubled. There were improvements in the soil, and the farmers earned more money. The study concluded that organic farming offered Africa great hope for breaking the cycle of poverty and hunger.

Farming in Africa

A. Read each statement. Circle **yes** if it is true or **no** if it is false. Use the information on the other page to help you.

1. Eighty percent of farmers in Africa are smallholder farmers.　　**Yes**　**No**

2. Most smallholder farmers in Africa are men.　　**Yes**　**No**

3. Examples of staple foods include corn, rice, and wheat.　　**Yes**　**No**

4. Smallholder farmers sell most of their crops to large food companies to be exported.　　**Yes**　**No**

5. Burning fields was a common practice on African farms.　　**Yes**　**No**

6. Organic farmers rotate their crops so that many different plants can be planted in the same soil.　　**Yes**　**No**

7. Many of the small farms in Africa are about 50 acres.　　**Yes**　**No**

8. The total amount of crops produced by African organic farming has increased.　　**Yes**　**No**

9. Organic farmers use chemical fertilizers to help their crops grow.　　**Yes**　**No**

10. Smallholder farmers produce 50% of the staple foods in Africa.　　**Yes**　**No**

B. Name three ways that changing to organic farming has helped smallholder farmers.

1. _____

_____

2. _____

_____

3. _____

_____

Sharing the Nile River

The Nile River is the longest river in Africa and in the world. Many streams and small rivers drain into the Nile, forming an area of land called the Nile Basin. The Nile Basin covers about one-tenth of the continent. It includes portions of Tanzania, Burundi, Rwanda, Democratic Republic of the Congo, Kenya, Uganda, Ethiopia, Eritrea, Republic of South Sudan, Sudan, and Egypt. Almost 300 million people live in the 11 countries that share the river.

In recent years, the use of the Nile's water has caused conflict among the 11 Nile Basin countries. Until recently, Egypt and Sudan had exclusive rights over the river—meaning they were the only countries who could control its water. They built dams and used the water to irrigate their farmland. They also used the Nile to generate electrical power. The Nile is the sole source of water for Egypt, Sudan, and Republic of South Sudan.

Other countries such as Kenya, Uganda, and Tanzania have argued that Egypt and Sudan need to share more of the waters of the Nile. Because of their concerns, an organization called the Nile Basin Initiative was formed. People from the 10 countries meet regularly to discuss solutions and ways to cooperate.

Nile River Basin

![Map of the Nile River Basin showing Mediterranean Sea, Nile River, Egypt, Sudan, Eritrea, Republic of South Sudan, Ethiopia, Uganda, Rwanda, Kenya, Democratic Republic of the Congo, Burundi, Tanzania, and Indian Ocean]

Sharing the Nile River

A. Fill in the blanks with the correct answers. Use the information and map on the other page to help you.

1. The Nile Basin covers about how much of Africa?   _____

2. How many countries are part of the Nile Basin?   _____

3. Until recently, which two countries controlled use   _____
   of the Nile River?

   _____

4. The Nile River flows north from Lake Victoria   _____
   and empties into what body of water?

5. What is the Nile Basin?

   _____

   _____

6. Why was the Nile Basin Initiative formed?

   _____

   _____

B. Name two ways people use the waters of the Nile.

1. _____

2. _____

C. On the Nile River Basin map on the other page, color the Nile River blue.
Then outline the edges of the Nile River Basin in green.

Cacao and Coffee

Cacao beans come from large pods that grow on the cacao tree. Cacao beans are used to make chocolate and cocoa. Every year, over 3 million tons (2.7 metric tons) of cacao beans are produced in the world. About 70% of the world's cacao beans are produced in African countries.

The country of Côte d'Ivoire is the world's leading cacao bean producer. Ghana is the third-largest cacao bean producer in the world. Nigeria and Cameroon rank fourth and sixth in the world, respectively.

Top African Cacao Producers

	Country	Amount Produced Yearly
1	Côte d'Ivoire	1,510,166 tons (1,370,000 metric tons)
2	Ghana	771,618 tons (700,000 metric tons)
3	Nigeria	551,156 tons (500,000 metric tons)
4	Cameroon	206,715 tons (187,532 metric tons)

Food and Agriculture Organization of the U.N. 2008

cacao plant

Coffee is a drink made from the roasted and ground beans of the coffee plant. Farmers pick the berries off the coffee plant. Each berry contains two beans that are dried and processed.

Ethiopia is Africa's leading producer of coffee. It is also the fifth-largest producer of coffee in the world.

Top African Coffee Producers

	Country	Amount Produced Yearly
1	Ethiopia	301,372 tons (273,400 metric tons)
2	Uganda	233,388 tons (211,726 metric tons)
3	Côte d'Ivoire	88,185 tons (80,000 metric tons)
4	Tanzania	47,510 tons (43,100 metric tons)

Food and Agriculture Organization of the U.N. 2008

coffee plant

Cacao and Coffee

Read each clue below. Write the correct word on the numbered lines. Then use the numbers to crack the code!

1. Cameroon ranks fourth in ____ production in Africa.

   __ __ __ __ __
   3 1 3 1 12

2. ____ is Africa's top producer of coffee.

   __ __ __ __ __ __ __ __
   5 15 8 9 12 13 9 1

3. Côte d'Ivoire is the world's ____ cacao producer.

   __ __ __ __ __ __ __
   10 5 1 4 9 11 7

4. ____ ranks second in Africa in production of coffee.

   __ __ __ __ __ __
   16 7 1 11 4 1

5. Cacao trees produce pods that contain cacao ____.

   __ __ __ __ __
   2 5 1 11 14

6. ____ is a drink made from the roasted and ground beans of a plant.

   __ __ __ __ __ __
   3 12 6 6 5 5

Crack the Code!

The average American eats 12 pounds (5.4 kg) of ____ per year!

__ __ __ __ __ __ __ __ __
3 8 12 3 12 10 1 15 5

African Safaris

Africa is a continent rich in wildlife. It is home to a wide variety of animals that range from large carnivores, such as the lion and leopard, to huge herbivores, such as the elephant and giraffe. In fact, some of the biggest animal species on the planet live in Africa. Adventurers and animal-lovers go on *safaris,* or overland journeys, to see these animals in person.

In the early 20th century, African safaris were popular with hunters seeking big game, such as Cape buffalo, elephant, leopard, lion, and rhinoceros. These animals were called the "big five" because they were the most dangerous to hunt. However, safari hunting took its toll on the wildlife population. Elephants, often hunted for their tusks, have had a 50% decrease in their population over the last 40 years. And the rhinoceros population has dwindled to only 10% of what it was 30 years ago.

Animals that were once hunted for horns, skins, and furs are now a different kind of valuable resource for Africa. Today, African safaris are often called eco-tours, short for ecological tourism. Tourists from all over the world come to Africa to learn more about the animals and to watch them in their natural habitat. Hunting is not allowed on these safaris. Africa's economy benefits from the money brought in by the eco-tours, and some of the money also goes to wildlife conservation programs.

Answer the questions. Use the information above to help you.

1. Which animals were considered the "big five" for hunting on safaris?

   _____

2. How have safaris changed since the early 20th century?

   _____

   _____

3. How does Africa's wildlife serve as a valuable resource today?

   _____

   _____

African Safaris

Many African animals now live in protected areas, such as nature preserves and national parks. People go on safaris in these areas to see wildlife in its natural habitat.

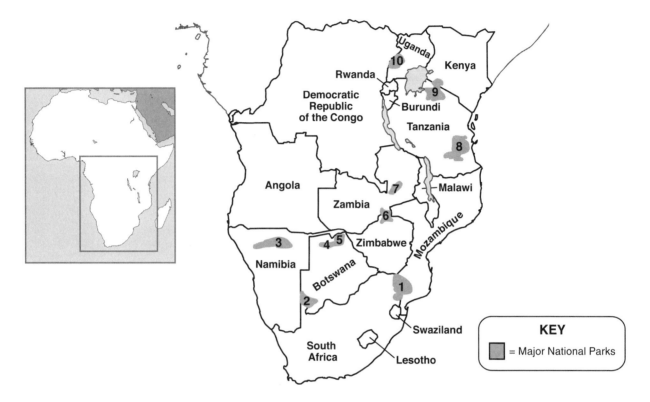

	Major National Parks
1	Kruger National Park
2	Kgalagadi Transfrontier Park
3	Etosha National Park
4	Moremi Wildlife Reserve
5	Chobe National Park
6	Lower Zambezi and Mana Pools National Parks
7	South Luangwa National Park
8	Selous Game Reserve
9	Serengeti/Masai Mara
10	Rwenzori National Park

The Great Migration

One of the sights that draws visitors to Eastern Africa is the "Great Migration." Visitors come to watch a megaherd of over 2 million grazing animals—mainly wildebeest, zebras, and gazelles—as they travel through the savanna.

Each year, the animals migrate in a circular path from the Serengeti Plains of Tanzania to the Masai Mara of Kenya and back again. They follow the rains that bring green grasses. Carnivores such as lions, hyenas, cheetahs, and leopards follow the herds and prey on the weak and the young.

The Great Migration Route

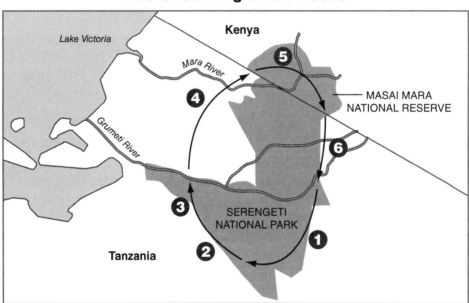

1 January–March: The megaherd is on the short-grass plains of the southern Serengeti. During this time, the wildebeest herds give birth to several hundred thousand calves.

2 April–May: The calves are strong enough to travel. The megaherd journeys northwest in search of food.

3 June: The herds must cross the crocodile-infested waters of the Grumeti River on their way north.

4 July–August: The herds move through the northern Serengeti toward the long-grass plains of the Masai Mara. They must cross another crocodile-filled river, the Mara.

5 September–October: The megaherd remains in the rich grasslands of the Mara until late October or early November.

6 November–December: The megaherd leaves the Mara and moves south toward the Serengeti. Here in the Serengeti Plains, the migration cycle begins once again.

The Great Migration

A. Next to each time period, write the letter of the migration event that takes place then. Use the information and map on the other page to help you.

_____ 1. January–March

_____ 2. June

_____ 3. July–August

_____ 4. September–October

_____ 5. April–May

_____ 6. November–December

a. The herds remain in the rich grasslands of the Mara.

b. The megaherd returns to the Serengeti Plains.

c. Wildebeest herds give birth to their calves.

d. The herds cross the crocodile-infested Grumeti River.

e. The megaherd and its calves journey northwest to find food.

f. The herds cross the Mara River to get to the Masai Mara.

B. Answer the questions, using the information on the other page.

1. About how many animals make up the megaherd of the Great Migration?

   _____

2. List the three main types of animals that are in the megaherd.

   _____

3. List the four types of carnivores that follow the megaherd to hunt.

   _____

4. Besides being hunted by carnivores, what other dangers might the herd encounter on its journey?

   _____

Africa's Desert Animals

Sahara Desert

The Sahara Desert in Northern Africa is home to many unusual animals. The dromedary, or one-humped camel, is a common sight in the desert. Venomous animals such as the deathstalker scorpion and the horned viper are dangerous predators that live in the Sahara. Brilliantly colored scarab beetles scurry on the desert ground and lay their eggs in animal dung. The endangered Saharan cheetah and a white antelope called the addax also make the Sahara their home.

fennec fox

One of the most unusual animals in the Sahara is the fennec fox. This fox is small, but it has very large ears. The bat-like ears radiate body heat and help keep the fox cool. Its long, thick hair—even on its feet—protects the animal from the hot sand.

Kalahari Desert

The Kalahari Desert in Southern Africa receives more rain than the other deserts of Africa. This attracts many animals to the region. Hyenas, desert lions, warthogs, jackals, and several species of antelope are found in the Kalahari. The ostrich, the largest bird in the world, also lives in the Kalahari.

An interesting animal of the Kalahari is the meerkat. Meerkats live in groups of up to 30 animals. The groups are called mobs. Throughout the day, adults take turns serving as lookouts and watching for predators. The other meerkats spend their day finding insects, lizards, birds, and eggs to eat. When an enemy is near, the lookout meerkat barks an alarm. The rest of the mob flees into its underground burrows.

meerkat

Namib Desert

The Namib Desert in southwestern Africa is barren and very dry. Most of the animals in this region are small. There are 70 species of lizards. One of the most unusual is the shovel-snouted lizard. It uses its snout to bury itself in the sand. The barking gecko and the golden blind mole are also found in the Namib Desert.

Sidewinder snakes, or adders, are venomous predators in the Namib Desert. The adder is able to climb sand dunes sideways, and only a small portion of its body ever touches the hot sand. The adder hunts by burying itself in the sand with only the tops of its eyes exposed. It lies there waiting to attack birds, lizards, or other snakes. When the prey is caught, the snake will swallow the animal headfirst.

adder

Africa's Desert Animals

A. Find and circle the desert animals in the word puzzle. Words may appear across, down, or diagonally.

```
A  D  D  X  T  A  D  D  E  R  N  U  E  E  X
E  B  S  C  O  R  P  L  N  I  D  A  E  E  B
U  O  C  A  R  B  C  N  A  R  F  L  C  F  A
Y  O  O  F  C  O  A  B  A  A  T  Q  J  E  C
L  W  R  T  S  U  V  Z  L  E  I  Z  Q  N  L
B  A  P  Z  T  E  I  F  E  Q  X  K  I  N  Z
T  V  I  A  K  L  C  B  T  B  S  V  T  E  X
R  M  O  M  E  E  R  V  I  P  C  I  R  C  L
E  O  N  M  M  E  E  R  K  A  T  O  Z  F  I
W  Q  T  Y  X  C  A  M  A  L  O  S  B  O  Z
B  A  V  A  Y  A  K  K  T  Q  R  T  E  X  K
V  C  D  R  O  M  E  D  H  M  P  R  A  C  T
Z  D  L  J  A  C  K  A  L  E  S  I  T  Z  H
A  E  T  H  C  B  E  R  V  E  N  C  K  B  P
B  S  D  R  O  M  E  D  A  R  Y  H  L  R  Q
```

addax

adder

beetle

dromedary

fennec fox

jackal

lizard

meerkat

ostrich

scorpion

B. Which desert animal from the other page would you most like to know more about? What did you find interesting about it? Explain your answer.

_____

_____

_____

_____

Rainforest Animals

The Mandrill

The mandrill is the largest of all monkeys. It lives in the rainforests of Western Africa. The mandrill has blue and red markings on its face. Its rump is also brightly colored. An adult mandrill is 3 feet (91 cm) tall, and it weighs 77 pounds (35 kg). It has extremely long canine teeth that can be used for self-defense.

mandrill monkey

Mandrills live in troops. The troop is headed by an adult male and includes 12 or more females and their young. Mandrills eat fruit, roots, insects, and small reptiles. They use their pouched cheeks to store food. Mandrills spend most of their time on the ground, but they do sleep in trees.

The Western Lowland Gorilla

The western lowland gorilla is one of the largest apes in the world. It lives in the rainforests of the Congo Basin. It has a standing height of 4 to 6 feet (1 to 2 m) and weighs 150 to 400 pounds (68 to 181 kg). It stays mostly on the ground, eating roots, fruit, tree bark, and pulp.

western lowland gorilla

Western lowland gorillas live in small troops of four to eight members. The troop is headed by one adult male called a silverback. He organizes troop activities and protects the troop. If challenged, the silverback will stand upright, throw things, act aggressively, and pound his chest while hooting loudly.

The Ruffed Lemur

There are 32 species of lemurs in the rainforests of Madagascar. The largest lemur is called the ruffed lemur. Most ruffed lemurs have a black and white coat with a fluffy white collar called a ruff. The ruffed lemur is about 20 inches long (50 cm) and weighs 7 to 12 pounds (3 to 5 kg). Its fluffy black tail is 24 inches (60 cm) long.

Ruffed lemurs live in groups of two to 16 animals. Adult females are dominant over males. Females defend the group, and food is given to them first. The group spends most of their time in the rainforest canopy. They feed on fruit, flowers, seeds, nectar, and leaves. When alarmed, the lemurs will roar loudly—a sound that can be heard over a mile away.

ruffed lemur

Rainforest Animals

A. Read each statement. Circle the correct animal that is described.

1. This animal lives in the Congo Basin.   **gorilla**   **mandrill**

2. The island of Madagascar is home to this animal.   **mandrill**   **lemur**

3. This animal has red and blue markings on its face.   **lemur**   **mandrill**

4. Females are in charge of this animal's group.   **lemur**   **gorilla**

5. The silverback is the leader of this troop.   **gorilla**   **lemur**

6. This animal eats plants and small reptiles.   **lemur**   **mandrill**

7. This animal can weigh 400 pounds (181 kg).   **gorilla**   **lemur**

8. The rainforest canopy is home to this animal.   **mandrill**   **lemur**

B. Draw a picture of a mandrill, lowland gorilla, or ruffed lemur. Write a caption next to the picture. Use the pictures and information on the other page to help you.

Review

Use words from the box to complete the crossword puzzle.

| cacao |
| diamonds |
| gorilla |
| meerkat |
| Nile |
| oil |
| safaris |
| wildebeest |

Across

3. Coffee and _____ are important crops in Africa.

4. Algeria is the top producer of _____ in Africa.

7. Ten African countries depend on the _____ River.

8. People go on _____ to see African wildlife in its natural habitat.

Down

1. Gold and _____ are valuable mineral resources of Africa.

2. Great herds of _____ migrate through the Serengeti.

5. The western lowland _____ lives in the Congo Basin.

6. The _____ lives in groups called mobs.

African Culture

This section introduces students to a wide variety of traditional African cultures. Students learn about the cultural importance of the arts and crafts made by different African tribes. They become familiar with traditional African music and dance, and learn how these have influenced modern musical trends. Students get a "taste" of common foods that are eaten on the continent. They find out that there are over 2,000 different languages and three major religious groups in Africa. Students also discover that the pyramids and the Sphinx of ancient Egypt are among the most famous tourist attractions in Africa.

Each skill in this section is based on the following National Geography Standards:

Essential Element 2: Places and Regions

Standard 6: How culture and experience influence people's perceptions of places and regions

Essential Element 4: Human Systems

Standard 10: The characteristics, distribution, and complexity of Earth's cultural mosaics

CONTENTS

Overview

The culture of a group of people consists of their beliefs, customs, and traditions. Culture is displayed in people's artwork, languages, religions, and architecture. The rich diversity of African cultures reflects the vastness of the continent.

Tourist Attractions

The most famous historical and cultural tourist attractions in Africa come from the ruins of ancient Egypt. The pyramids outside the city of Giza are thousands of years old. The giant statue of the Sphinx guards the pharaohs' ancient tombs. Each year millions of tourists visit these sites.

Arts and Crafts

Traditional arts and crafts are an important means of expression for many tribes in Africa. Skilled craftspeople create works of art from wood, stone, leather, and fabric. Spears, ceremonial masks for religious and cultural events, and detailed figures of humans and animals are carved from wood and stone. Decorative leather shields are made to represent tribal groups, and colorful woven fabrics tell stories through their beautiful designs and details.

Music and Dance

Traditional African songs and dances help maintain the oral traditions of many different cultural groups. Musicians play instruments such as the *djembe,* which is a West African drum, the *balafon* (xylophone), and the *sansa* (thumb piano).

Languages

More than 2,000 languages are spoken in Africa. They are divided into six language families: Afro-Asian, Nilo-Saharan, Niger-Congo, Khoisan, Austronesian, and Indo-European.

Religions

Islam and Christianity are two major religions practiced in Africa. Traditional African religions are also observed. Daily life in Africa is greatly influenced by the religious beliefs of its people.

Cuisines

Many Africans eat their largest meal at lunchtime. Hearty soups and stews are served, along with rice, vegetables such as cassava and yams, and fruits such as plantains. The countries of Morocco, Nigeria, Ethiopia, Republic of the Congo, and South Africa are famous for their special regional cuisines.

Overview

Fill in the bubble to answer each question or complete each sentence.

1. The Pyramids of Giza are located in which African country?
   - Ⓐ Egypt
   - Ⓑ Ghana
   - Ⓒ Nigeria
   - Ⓓ South Africa

2. Which of these hand-crafted objects was *not* mentioned on the other page?
   - Ⓐ wooden masks
   - Ⓑ leather shields
   - Ⓒ woven fabrics
   - Ⓓ metal jewelry

3. A drum called the ____ is used to play African music.
   - Ⓐ kora
   - Ⓑ djembe
   - Ⓒ sansa
   - Ⓓ balafon

4. Two major religions in Africa are Islam and ____.
   - Ⓐ Buddhism
   - Ⓑ Hinduism
   - Ⓒ Christianity
   - Ⓓ Judaism

5. Which statement is true about the languages of Africa?
   - Ⓐ In Africa, there are five large language families.
   - Ⓑ English is the most popular language in Africa.
   - Ⓒ There are more than 2,000 languages in Africa.
   - Ⓓ There are more than 1,000 Afro-Asian languages in Africa.

Tourist Attractions

About 4,500 years ago, the Egyptian people built great pyramids as tombs for their *pharaohs,* or kings. Many kings and queens were buried in these pyramids. The ruins of 35 major pyramids still stand near the Nile River in Egypt. The most famous pyramids are located on the west bank of the Nile near a city called Giza. There are 10 pyramids at Giza, the three largest of which are the best preserved.

Pyramids of Giza

Every year, millions of visitors travel to Egypt to see the magnificent pyramids. Visitors can walk or ride horses and camels around the complex of pyramids. If *archaeologists* (people who study artifacts of the past) are not working on a tomb, visitors are sometimes allowed to enter one of the pyramids.

The Great Pyramid

The Great Pyramid is the largest and oldest of the preserved pyramids. The Great Pyramid was built for King Khufu (KOO-foo) in about 2,500 BC. It was originally 481 feet (147 m) tall, but some of the upper stones are now gone. Today, it stands 450 feet (137 m) tall. Originally, the pyramid's outer surface was smooth and white. It was built with more than 2 million limestone blocks, weighing 2½ to 15 tons (2.3 to 13.6 metric tons) each. Thousands of workers moved these huge stone blocks without the help of modern machines.

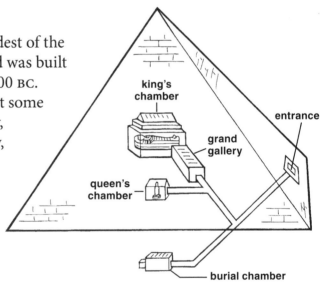

The Great Pyramid has three burial chambers. The first one is deep underground. The second is aboveground and is called the queen's chamber. However, it was never intended to be a burial chamber for Khufu's wives. Experts think that it housed a statue of the king. The grand gallery leads to the third burial chamber—the king's chamber. This chamber held a red granite *sarcophagus,* or coffin, placed in the center of the pyramid. King Khufu was buried in the sarcophagus.

Tourist Attractions

The Pyramid of Khafre

The second-largest pyramid at Giza was built for King Khafre (KAF-ray), the son of King Khufu. The pyramid stands on higher ground, so it appears to be taller than the Great Pyramid. Originally, it stood 471 feet (144 m) high. Now it stands 446 feet (136 m) tall. The base of the pyramid covers about 11 acres.

King Khafre's pyramid is the only one at Giza that has some of its original layer of smooth, white outer stones. There is evidence that 58 statues once stood in and around the pyramid. The statues included animals and life-size figures of the pharaoh.

King Khafre

The Pyramid of Menkaure

The third-largest pyramid at Giza was built for King Menkaure (men-KOO-ray), the grandson of King Khufu. It originally stood 215 feet (66 m) high. Now it is 203 feet (62 m) high. Menkaure's pyramid was more expensive to build. Instead of the typical limestone, the pyramid walls were covered in granite, a stronger and less abundant rock than limestone.

Menkaure's tomb was opened in the 1800s. The sarcophagus was supposed to be sent to England. However, the ship carrying it sank in the Mediterranean Sea, and the ancient treasure was lost.

an example of a sarcophagus fit for a pharaoh

The Queens' Pyramids

Besides the three large pyramids, a number of smaller pyramids stand at Giza. There are three queens' pyramids near the Great Pyramid of Khufu. They lie in a row along the east side of the Great Pyramid. Each one is about one-fifth the size of the Great Pyramid.

Egyptologists (archaeologists who study Egyptian history, language, literature, and art) are not certain which women were buried inside, since all three bodies are gone. One pyramid is believed to have been the tomb of Khufu's mother.

There are also three queens' pyramids alongside Menkaure's pyramid.

the Queens' Pyramids

Tourist Attractions

The millions of people who visit the pyramids at Giza also come to see the world-famous landmark called the Great Sphinx.

The Story of the Sphinx

A sphinx is a mythological creature with the body of a lion and the head of a human. Ancient Egyptian art showed kings as sphinxes conquering their enemies. The sphinx became the symbol for royal protection, and Egyptians made statues of sphinxes to honor a king or queen.

The Great Sphinx has the head of a man and the body, feet, and tail of a lion. It also wears a royal headdress. Although it is one of the world's oldest and largest statues, there is debate about who the statue was made for and exactly when it was built. Many historians believe that the head of the Great Sphinx is that of King Khafre. That is because the monument is located near the king's pyramid.

The head and body of the Great Sphinx were carved out of a gigantic limestone block. Smaller blocks of stone were used for the paws and legs. The sculpture is 240 feet (73 m) long and 66 feet (20 m) high. That is as tall as a six-story building! One distinctive feature of the Sphinx is that its nose is missing. Some people think the head was used as target practice by conquering soldiers, and that is why it is badly damaged.

Sand has often buried the Great Sphinx up to its neck. Over the years, wind, rain, and sun have also worn away the stone. Since the 1980s, scientists have made great efforts to try to save the crumbling stone. They hope the ancient monument will be preserved for its historical importance to Africa and the world.

Name _____

Tourist Attractions

A. Read each statement. Circle the correct term, monument, or person that is described.

1. The Egyptians built these tombs for their kings.

   pyramids   **sphinxes**

2. The pyramids were built near this city.

   Cairo   **Giza**

3. This is a special name for an Egyptian ruler.

   king   **pharaoh**

4. Pyramids were built mostly of this kind of rock.

   limestone   **granite**

5. A king or queen was buried in this special coffin.

   gallery   **sarcophagus**

6. This pharaoh had the Great Pyramid built.

   King Khafre   **King Khufu**

7. This king's coffin was lost at sea.

   King Menkaure   **King Khufu**

8. This huge sculpture wears a royal headdress.

   Queen's Pyramid   **Great Sphinx**

9. A sphinx has the body of this animal.

   lion   **tiger**

10. The Great Sphinx was most likely built for this king.

    King Khafre   **King Menkaure**

B. Would you like to visit the monuments of Giza? Why or why not?

_____

_____

_____

Arts and Crafts

For thousands of years, African artists have created objects that are both beautiful and useful for everyday life. This is an important tradition in African culture.

African Masks

African masks are one of the most widely recognized art forms on the continent. They are made by various African tribes who each create their masks a little differently. Materials such as wood, metal, leather, and fabric are used to create the masks. Carved wooden masks are often decorated with paint, shells, plant fibers, and horns.

Historically, masks have been worn during harvest festivals, religious ceremonies, and battles. The masks represented spirits of the tribes' dead ancestors. They also depicted mythical creatures and animal spirits. Today, African masks are still considered sacred objects. Traditional masks are also displayed in museums throughout Africa and the world as objects of fine art.

Animal mask from the Dogon tribe of Mali

Shields and Spears

In Africa, many tribes make beautifully designed tools and weapons. The Zulu people of South Africa and the Maasai of Tanzania have created leather shields for centuries. A Maasai warrior is rarely seen without a spear and shield. The Maasai use the weapons to protect their cattle from lion attacks. A warrior's shield is made of Cape buffalo hide and decorated with paint. Spears are also used as walking sticks. The spears are made from ebony wood and metal.

Shield and spear from the Maasai tribe of Tanzania

Sculptures

Sculpture is an important African art form. In ancient times, clay was used to create human and animal figures. Later, brass and bronze were cast to make sculptures. Figures were also carved out of wood and ivory.

Today, many cultural groups continue the art of sculpture carving. The Makonde tribe of Tanzania are master ebony woodcarvers. Other cultural groups use stone for carving. Natural stone is used in both its rough, textured state and in a highly polished form to show the rich colors. The Kisii tribe of Kenya and the Shona of Zimbabwe are known for sculpting human and animal figures out of a rock called soapstone.

Soapstone sculpture from the Kisii tribe of Kenya

Arts and Crafts

Complete each sentence by unscrambling the word under the line. Use the information on the other page to help you.

1. People wore masks to represent their dead ancestors, mythical creatures,

   and _____ spirits.
   lamina

2. Historically, tribes wore masks during religious _____.
   cernomeise

3. Most Maasai shields are made out of _____.
   erlateh

4. A Maasai warrior usually carries a shield and a _____.
   ersap

5. The Shona people use _____ to carve figures.
   sneotpaos

6. Spears are made from _____ wood and metal.
   ynoeb

7. _____ and animal figures are sculpted from wood and stone.
   munha

8. Traditional African art objects are displayed in art galleries and

   _____ throughout the world.
   smusemu

9. Carved wooden masks are often decorated with horns, shells, plant fibers,

   and _____.
   tapin

10. Brass and _____ are metals used in African sculptures.
    onberz

Three African Fabrics

African clothing is recognized around the world for its bold patterns and colors. Three kinds of fabric—adinkra, kente, and bogolanfini—have special meaning to the people who make and wear them.

Adinkra

Adinkra is a printed or stamped cotton cloth. It is made by the Ashanti people of Ghana. The cloth is divided into boxes drawn with black dye made from tree bark. Symbols are stamped onto the cloth. There are about 100 different symbols, each with its own meaning. A carver cuts the stamps out of the bottom of a *calabash,* which is a type of gourd. Each stamp is dipped in the dye and pressed onto the cloth in patterns to tell a story.

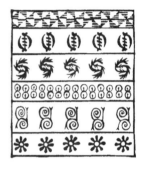

At one time, adinkra cloth was worn only for funerals. Today, garments made from adinkra cloth are used for other special occasions, such as weddings and births.

Kente

Kente is another kind of cloth made by the Ashanti people. It is made from thin strips of cloth that are woven on narrow looms. The strips are then carefully arranged and hand-sewn together to make a garment. There are over 300 different designs. Colors are chosen for their symbolic meanings. For example, blue means love and harmony, green means growth and health, and white means purity and balance.

Originally, kente cloth was worn only by royalty or for important social and religious occasions. Today, kente cloth is the most popular and best known of all African fabrics.

Bogolanfini

Bogolanfini is a mud cloth that is made by the Bamara people of Mali. Cotton is hand-spun and then woven into long strips on a loom. The strips are sewn together. Then the cloth is soaked in a special solution made from pounded leaves of the bogolon tree, which turns the cloth a yellow color. A dye made from iron-rich mud is later applied in lines, circles, zigzags, and oval shapes. The final step is bleaching. A soda solution is applied to the yellow area of the cloth where the mud dye was not applied. The solution bleaches the cloth from yellow to white.

The geometric designs of mud cloth stand out on its white background. Each piece of mud cloth tells a story. No two pieces are alike, and every pattern has a meaning.

Three African Fabrics

A. Fill in the blanks using the information on the other page to help you.

African _____ are often made using natural materials.

Bogolanfini, or _____ cloth, is dyed with a solution made

from pounded _____. Adinkra cloth designs are stamped

with dye made from _____. The stamps are cut from

a _____, which is a type of gourd.

The designs and colors of African fabrics are significant. Each symbol on

an adinkra cloth has its own _____. The pattern formed by

the symbols tells a _____. The colors of kente cloth are

symbolic, too. For example, green means growth and _____,

while _____ means purity and balance. And the lines,

circles, and other shapes that decorate a bogolanfini cloth have special meaning

as well. Because of these _____ patterns, no two pieces

of mud cloth are alike.

B. Match the name of the cloth with its definition.

_____ 1. adinkra

_____ 2. bogolanfini

_____ 3. kente

a. a mud cloth with geometric designs, made by the Bamara people of Mali

b. a colorful cloth that is made by the Ashanti people of Ghana and has more than 300 different designs

c. a cloth that has special stamped symbols, made by the Ashanti people of Ghana

Music and Dance

Music is a part of everyday life in Africa. African music has influenced different styles of music in the United States and elsewhere throughout the world. Jazz, rhythm and blues, gospel music, rock and roll, and hip hop all have roots in African rhythms. African music is unique in that it joins two or more rhythms within a song.

Traditional Singing

Most African songs have been passed down through many generations. The musical form of most songs in Africa is "call and response." One musician leads a melody or chant with a call and the others repeat or respond to the call.

Musical Instruments

A wide variety of instruments are used in African music. In particular, there are many types of drums in different shapes and sizes. The *djembe* (JEM-bay) drum of West Africa is probably the most recognizable. There are also stringed instruments such as musical bows and the *kora*, which is a type of harp. A thumb piano called a *sansa* comes from Angola. It is a small instrument with metal keys that are plucked using the thumbs. A West African *balafon*, which is like a xylophone, is another popular type of instrument. There is also a large variety of trumpets, horns, rattles, and bells.

African Dance

In African traditions, movement is regarded as an important form of communication. African dance movements may be simple, emphasizing the upper body, torso, or feet. The movements can also be complicated, involving coordination of several different body parts. The dancers move to express their feelings and to match the multiple beats of drums and other instruments.

Music and Dance

Read each clue below. Write the correct word on the numbered lines. Then use the numbers to crack the code!

1. Call and _____ is an African form of song.

   $\overline{5}$ $\overline{15}$ $\overline{4}$ $\overline{6}$ $\overline{7}$ $\overline{8}$ $\overline{4}$ $\overline{15}$

2. A sansa is the name for a thumb _____.

   $\overline{6}$ $\overline{12}$ $\overline{18}$ $\overline{8}$ $\overline{7}$

3. One kind of African xylophone is called a _____.

   $\overline{17}$ $\overline{18}$ $\overline{10}$ $\overline{18}$ $\overline{14}$ $\overline{7}$ $\overline{8}$

4. A djembe is a West African _____.

   $\overline{16}$ $\overline{5}$ $\overline{2}$ $\overline{9}$

5. A _____ is a stringed instrument similar to a harp.

   $\overline{11}$ $\overline{7}$ $\overline{5}$ $\overline{18}$

6. Multiple _____ are used in traditional African music.

   $\overline{5}$ $\overline{13}$ $\overline{1}$ $\overline{3}$ $\overline{13}$ $\overline{9}$ $\overline{4}$

Crack the Code!

In other parts of Africa, the sansa is called a _____.

$\overline{9}$ $\overline{17}$ $\overline{12}$ $\overline{5}$ $\overline{18}$

Languages of Africa

More than 2,000 languages are spoken in Africa. That's nearly one-third of the number of languages spoken in the entire world! Every country has official and unofficial languages that are spoken by different cultural groups.

The major language groups spoken in Africa are shown on the map.

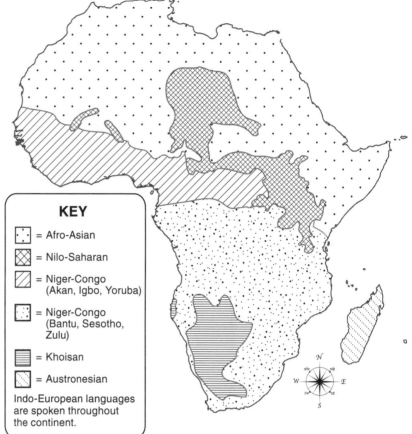

KEY

⬚ = Afro-Asian

⬚ = Nilo-Saharan

⬚ = Niger-Congo (Akan, Igbo, Yoruba)

⬚ = Niger-Congo (Bantu, Sesotho, Zulu)

⬚ = Khoisan

⬚ = Austronesian

Indo-European languages are spoken throughout the continent.

Afro-Asian languages are spoken throughout Northern Africa. This includes about 370 different languages. The two main ones are Arabic and Berber. More Africans speak Arabic than any other language.

Nilo-Saharan languages are spoken in parts of Central and Eastern Africa. There are nearly 200 of these languages, including Bari, Dinka, Kalenjin, Kanuri, and Maa.

Niger-Congo languages make up the largest language family, with over 1,400 languages. The Niger-Congo languages of Western and Central Africa include Akan, Igbo, and Yoruba. The Niger-Congo languages spoken in Central, Eastern, and Southern Africa include 500 Bantu languages, especially Swahili, which is the most widely spoken Bantu language. Other languages of Southern Africa are Sesotho and Zulu.

Khoisan languages of Southern Africa are called "click languages" because many words are expressed with unique clicking sounds made with the tongue. There are only 35 Khoisan languages.

Austronesian languages are spoken on Madagascar. Malagasy is the main language.

Indo-European languages, such as English, French, Portuguese, and Spanish, are also spoken throughout Africa. In South Africa, 13% of the population speaks Afrikaans, a language that comes from the Dutch, with influences from a number of other languages.

Languages of Africa

A. Answer the questions. Use the information and map on the other page to help you.

1. About how many languages are spoken in Africa? _____

2. Africa has how many major language groups? _____

3. Which of the major language groups is the largest? _____

4. What is the most widely spoken of the 500 Bantu languages? _____

5. The languages of Bari, Dinka, and Maa belong to which major language group? _____

6. In which country is the language of Malagasy spoken? _____

7. Which two major languages are spoken in Northern Africa?

   _____

8. Why are the Khoisan languages sometimes called "click languages"?

   _____

9. What are the two major language groups spoken in Southern Africa?

   _____

10. Name four European languages that are spoken in Africa.

   _____

B. On the map on the other page, color each major language area a different color. On the key, color each square to match the colors you used on the map.

Major Religions of Africa

Christianity, Islam, and many traditional African religions are practiced in Africa. Islam is the most popular religion, followed by Christianity. But many African people identify with more than one religion. It is common for Africans to follow Islam or Christianity but also to retain beliefs and practices from their traditional African religions.

Number of Followers of Major Religions in Africa

	Traditional African	Islam	Christianity
Northern Africa	9,000,000	167,000,000	6,000,000
Western Africa	42,000,000	130,000,000	67,000,000
Central Africa	21,000,000	14,000,000	62,000,000
Eastern Africa	52,000,000	59,000,000	135,000,000
Southern Africa	14,000,000	872,000	34,000,000
Total	**138,000,000**	**370,872,000**	**304,000,000**
Percentage of All Africans	**17%**	**45%**	**37%**

Figures are from "Spread of Christianity and Islam in Africa" from the *Western Journal of Black Studies*, 2005. Numbers have been rounded.

Traditional African

There are hundreds of traditional African religions. That is because each ethnic group has its own set of beliefs and practices. However, these religions have many things in common. Most traditional African religions explain how the universe was created. They also teach what is right and wrong and recognize the existence of a supreme god. People pray and make offerings to spirits of dead ancestors to bring blessings upon their families.

Islam

Islam is practiced throughout Africa. It began in the Middle East, spreading through Northern Africa and other regions. Islam is based on the teachings of the prophet Muhammad. The basic belief is that there is only one God, Allah. Muslims, or followers of Islam, have five major duties. They must declare their faith, pray five times a day, give money to charity, fast during the month of Ramadan, and travel to Muhammad's birthplace of Mecca, Saudi Arabia, once in their lifetime.

Christianity

Christianity is the other major religion practiced in Africa. Christianity was spread throughout Africa by missionaries from Europe and North America. Christians believe that there is only one God and that his son, Jesus Christ, was sent to Earth to save them from sin. Christians are taught to follow the Ten Commandments found in the Bible.

Major Religions of Africa

A. Read each statement. Circle **yes** if it is true or **no** if it is false. Use the information on the other page to help you.

1. There are hundreds of traditional religions practiced in Africa. **Yes   No**

2. Many African people identify with more than one religion. **Yes   No**

3. There are many different traditional religions in Africa because each group has its own set of beliefs and practices. **Yes   No**

4. Most Africans are Christians. **Yes   No**

5. The religion of Islam is practiced by 45% of Africans. **Yes   No**

6. In traditional African religions, families pray for blessings from the spirits of their dead ancestors. **Yes   No**

7. About 138 million people practice Christianity in Africa. **Yes   No**

8. More people practice traditional African religions in Eastern Africa than in any other region. **Yes   No**

9. Northern Africa has the highest number of Muslims. **Yes   No**

10. More people practice Christianity in Southern Africa than in any other region. **Yes   No**

B. Fill in the chart below, ranking the religions based on how many followers they have in Africa. Number **1** should have the most followers. Use the information on the other page to help you.

Rank	Religion	Total Number of Followers	Percentage
1			
2			
3			

African Cuisines

The meals that Africans eat on a daily basis vary by region and country. Every country grows different kinds of foods that influence the local cuisine.

Typically, breakfast in Africa is a light meal eaten very early. Porridge, bean cakes, boiled yams, and plantains are common breakfast foods. Many Africans eat a large meal at lunch—any time from noon to 4 PM. Hearty, spicy soups and stews are served along with grains, vegetables, and fruits. Dinner is eaten any time from 5 PM to 10 PM in Africa. It is a light meal, often consisting of leftovers from lunch.

The chart below highlights five countries, one from each region of Africa, and some foods that are commonly eaten there.

Country	Favorite Foods
Morocco (Northern Africa)	• *Tagine* is a Moroccan stew that can be served different ways. Two varieties are tagine of lamb with prunes, and tagine of chicken with lentils. • Couscous, which is a crushed, steamed grain, is often served with lamb or chicken in a spicy sauce. • Dates with an almond paste filling or pastries with orange-flower custard and berries are often served for dessert.
Nigeria (Western Africa)	• *Efo,* a spinach soup, and groundnut stew are popular dishes. (Peanuts are called groundnuts in Western Africa.) • *Jollof* rice is a combination of boiled rice, tomatoes, onions, and hot spices. Chicken is often added to the spicy red dish. • *Dodo* are fried plantains, or West African bananas. They are eaten for breakfast or as a snack.
Ethiopia (Eastern Africa)	• *Wat* is a rich stew that is prepared with vegetables, chicken, or beef and seasoned with spices. • Most Ethiopian stews also contain *berbere,* a thick red paste made of 14 different spices blended with water and oil. • *Injera* is a spongy, sour flatbread that is used to scoop up and wrap food instead of using utensils.
Republic of the Congo (Central Africa)	• *Mwamba* is a basic stew that is made with chicken, beef, fish, or lamb and spiced with red pepper. • Stews are served with rice or *fufu.* Fufu is mashed cooked corn or *cassava* (a root vegetable) that is formed into a ball. Fufu is used to scoop up the stew instead of utensils. • *Chikwange* is another dish served with stew. It is mashed cassava prepared with banana leaves.
South Africa (Southern Africa)	• *Bobotie* is a meatloaf made of beef or lamb with raisins and a baked egg. • Meats are served with *chutney,* a sweet fruit sauce. • *Samp* and beans is a staple for many South Africans. Samp is cracked or ground dried corn. Cowpeas (black-eyed peas) and samp are soaked in water and then cooked with onions, potatoes, and curry spice.

African Cuisines

A. Next to each type of food, write the letter of the definition that explains it.

_____ 1. berbere   a. a rich Ethiopian stew

_____ 2. chutney   b. a spongy flatbread from Ethiopia

_____ 3. dodo   c. a ball of mashed cooked corn or cassava

_____ 4. wat   d. a Moroccan stew

_____ 5. fufu   e. a thick red paste made with 14 spices

_____ 6. injera   f. a root vegetable

_____ 7. efo   g. a sweet fruit sauce

_____ 8. samp   h. a Nigerian spinach soup

_____ 9. tagine   i. fried plantains, or bananas

_____ 10. cassava   j. cracked corn that is cooked with beans

B. Make a menu of African dishes that you would like to serve for dinner. Be sure to include a main course, a side dish to accompany the main dish, and a dessert. Describe each dish and write its country of origin.

Main Course (stew, soup, or meat dish)	Description	Country
Second Course (side dish)		
Third Course (dessert)		

Review

Use words from the box to complete the crossword puzzle.

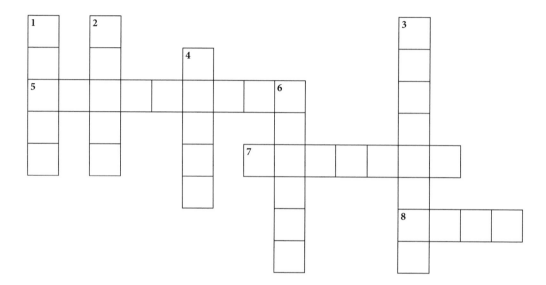

dodo

Islam

kente

languages

masks

pyramids

rhythms

Sphinx

Across

5. There are more than 2,000 _____ in Africa.

7. African music has many complicated _____.

8. fried plantains, or West African bananas

Down

1. a major religion in Africa

2. _____ cloth is the most popular African fabric.

3. The _____ of Giza are thousands of years old.

4. Wooden _____ are worn for religious and cultural events.

6. The Great _____ is a popular tourist attraction in Egypt.

Assessment

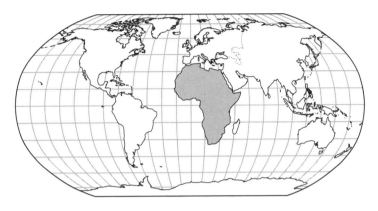

This section provides two cumulative assessments that you can use to evaluate students' acquisition of the information presented in this book. The first assessment requires students to identify selected cities, countries, landforms, and bodies of water on a combined physical and political map. The second assessment is a two-page multiple-choice test covering information from all sections of the book. Use one or both assessments as culminating activities for your class's study of Africa.

CONTENTS

Map Test

Write the name of the country, capital city, landform, or body of water that matches each number. Use the words in the box to help you.

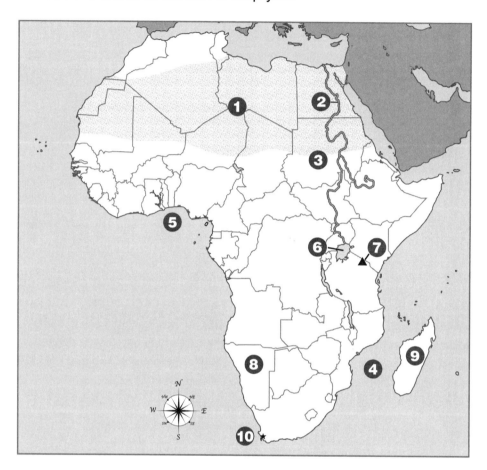

Sudan	Cape Town	Madagascar	Lake Victoria	Mozambique Channel
Namibia	Nile River	Gulf of Guinea	Sahara Desert	Mount Kilimanjaro

1. _____   6. _____

2. _____   7. _____

3. _____   8. _____

4. _____   9. _____

5. _____   10. _____

The 7 Continents: Africa • EMC 3737 • © Evan-Moor Corp.

Multiple-Choice Test

Fill in the bubble to answer each question or complete each sentence.

1. Africa is the second-largest continent in the world in ____.

   Ⓐ size

   Ⓑ population

   Ⓒ both size and population

   Ⓓ number of cities and countries

2. Which imaginary line runs horizontally through the center of Africa?

   Ⓐ equator

   Ⓑ prime meridian

   Ⓒ Tropic of Cancer

   Ⓓ Tropic of Capricorn

3. In which hemispheres is Africa located?

   Ⓐ Northern and Southern

   Ⓑ Eastern, Western, and Southern

   Ⓒ Northern, Southern, and Eastern

   Ⓓ all four hemispheres

4. Africa's ____ countries are divided into ____ regions.

   Ⓐ 25, 4

   Ⓑ 54, 5

   Ⓒ 65, 8

   Ⓓ 75, 10

5. Which African country is the largest in area?

   Ⓐ Chad

   Ⓑ Libya

   Ⓒ Sudan

   Ⓓ Algeria

6. Which country ranks first in population?

   Ⓐ Nigeria

   Ⓑ Ethiopia

   Ⓒ Tanzania

   Ⓓ South Africa

7. What is the highest point in Africa?

   Ⓐ Atlas Mountains

   Ⓑ Mount Kilimanjaro

   Ⓒ Ethiopian Highlands

   Ⓓ Great Rift Valley

8. The ____ Desert is the largest desert in Africa.

   Ⓐ Namib

   Ⓑ Nubian

   Ⓒ Sahara

   Ⓓ Kalahari

Multiple-Choice Test

9. What is the longest river in Africa and in the world?

   Ⓐ Nile River

   Ⓑ Niger River

   Ⓒ Congo River

   Ⓓ Zambezi River

10. The top two oil-producing countries in Africa are _____.

    Ⓐ Libya and Egypt

    Ⓑ Angola and Sudan

    Ⓒ Nigeria and Algeria

    Ⓓ Equatorial Guinea and Gabon

11. Gold and _____ are major minerals that are mined in Africa.

    Ⓐ topaz

    Ⓑ quartz

    Ⓒ feldspar

    Ⓓ diamonds

12. Which of these African animals can only be found in the rainforest?

    Ⓐ hyena

    Ⓑ gorilla

    Ⓒ fennec fox

    Ⓓ wildebeest

13. The Great Migration happens every year in which area?

    Ⓐ Serengeti Plains

    Ⓑ Rift Valley

    Ⓒ Sahara Desert

    Ⓓ Ethiopian Highlands

14. Which two major religions are the largest in Africa?

    Ⓐ Islam and Confucianism

    Ⓑ Judaism and Hinduism

    Ⓒ Islam and Christianity

    Ⓓ Buddhism and Christianity

15. There are more than _____ languages spoken in Africa.

    Ⓐ 1,000

    Ⓑ 2,000

    Ⓒ 3,000

    Ⓓ 5,000

16. The pyramids of Giza and the Great Sphinx are located in _____.

    Ⓐ Mali

    Ⓑ Benin

    Ⓒ Kenya

    Ⓓ Egypt

Note Takers

This section provides four note taker forms that give students the opportunity to culminate their study of Africa by doing independent research on places or animals of their choice. (Some suggested topics are given below.) Students may use printed reference materials or Internet sites to gather information on their topics. A cover page is also provided so that students may create a booklet of note takers and any other reproducible pages from the book that you would like students to save.

FORMS

Select a physical feature of Africa. Write notes about it to complete each section.

_____

(Name of Physical Feature)

Location

_____
_____
_____

Interesting Facts

_____
_____
_____
_____
_____
_____
_____
_____
_____
_____
_____
_____

Description

_____
_____
_____
_____
_____
_____
_____
_____
_____

Animals or Plants

_____
_____
_____

Name _____

Draw an African animal. Then write notes about it to complete each section.

_____

(Name of Animal)

Habitat

_____
_____
_____
_____

Endangered? (Yes) (No)

Physical Characteristics

_____
_____
_____

Diet

_____
_____
_____
_____

Behaviors

_____
_____
_____
_____

Enemies/Defenses

_____
_____
_____
_____

Name _____

Draw an African tourist attraction. Then write notes about it to complete each section.

_____
(Name of Tourist Attraction)

Location

_____
_____
_____

Description

_____
_____
_____
_____
_____
_____
_____
_____
_____

Interesting Facts

_____
_____
_____

Name _____

Select an African city you would like to visit. Write notes about it to complete each section.

My Trip to _____
(Name of City)

Location

_____

_____

_____

_____

How I Would Get There

_____

_____

_____

_____

Things I Would See and Do

_____

_____

_____

_____

_____

_____

_____

_____

Foods I Would Eat

_____

_____

_____

_____

Learning the Language

How to Say "Hello"

_____

How to Say "Goodbye"

_____

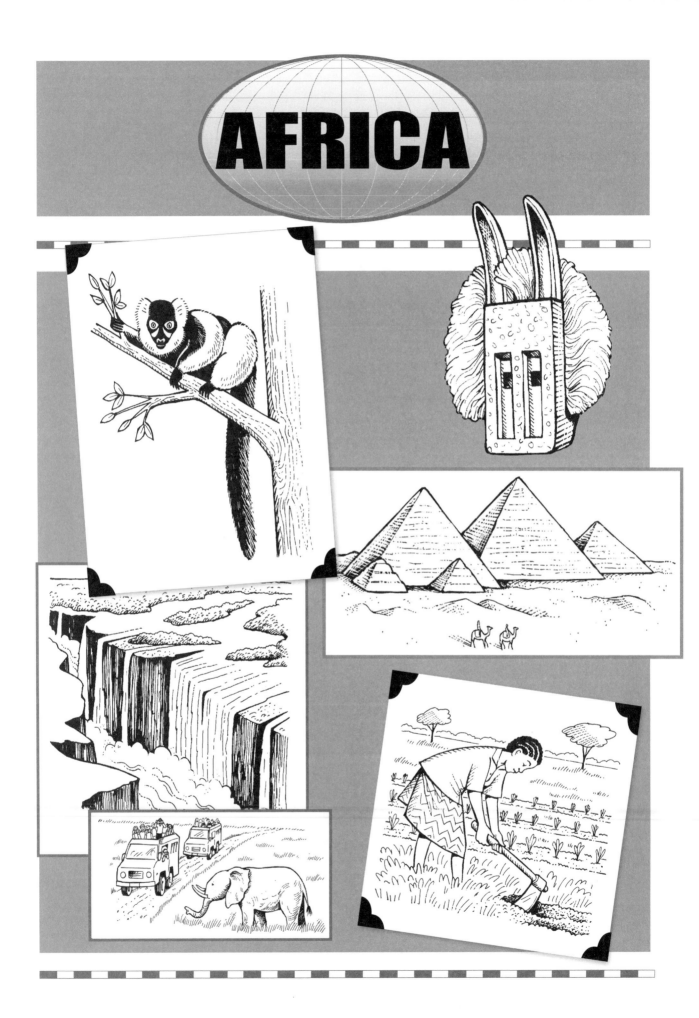

Page 5

1. C   2. A   3. B   4. D   5. B

Page 6

A. Europe, Antarctica, Asia, South America, Atlantic, east, Red, Mediterranean

B. 1. Students should color Europe red.
   2. Students should circle the label *Atlantic Ocean* with blue.
   3. Students should draw a panda on Asia.

Page 9

A. 1. c   4. e   7. a
   2. f   5. i   8. g
   3. h   6. b   9. d

B.

Page 11

A. 1. equator   6. latitude lines
   2. prime meridian   7. 15 degrees
   3. equator   8. parallels
   4. 15°E   9. 30°S
   5. 90°N   10. meridians

B. Egypt is located north of the equator and east of the prime meridian, so its latitude and longitude are labeled in degrees north and east.

Page 12

A. 1. Yes   5. Yes
   2. Yes   6. No
   3. No   7. No
   4. Yes   8. Yes

B. 3: Europe, Antarctica, and Africa

Page 14

Across   **Down**
3. second   1. prime
5. Asia   2. Indian
6. Atlantic   4. equator
7. four   5. Africa

Page 17

1. C   2. D   3. B   4. C   5. A

Page 18

A. Answers will vary—e.g., Yes, because it is projected to increase by 500 million every 20 years.

Page 19

B. 1. Yes   5. Yes   9. No
   2. Yes   6. No   10. No
   3. No   7. No
   4. Yes   8. Yes

C. 772 million

Page 22

A.

Rank	Country	Square Miles	Square Kilometers
1	Algeria	919,595	2,381,741
2	DRC	905,355	2,344,858
3	Sudan	718,720	1,861,484
4	Libya	679,360	1,759,540
5	Chad	496,000	1,284,000

Page 23

B. Student should color each country a different color and complete the map key.

The Five Largest Countries
1. Algeria   Color will vary.
2. DRC   Color will vary.
3. Sudan   Color will vary.
4. Libya   Color will vary.
5. Chad   Color will vary.

Page 24

A.

Rank	Country	Square Miles	Square Kilometers	Number of Main Islands
1	Seychelles	176	455	3
2	São Tomé	372	964	2
3	Comoros	719	1,862	3
4	Mauritius	788	2,040	1
5	Cape Verde	1,557	4,033	10

Page 25

B. Students should color each country a different color and complete the map key.

The Five Smallest Countries

1. Seychelles   Color will vary.
2. São Tomé and Príncipe Color will vary.
3. Comoros   Color will vary.
4. Mauritius   Color will vary.
5. Cape Verde   Color will vary.

Page 27

A. 1. 1
   2. Egypt
   3. 8
   4. Ethiopia
   5. Kenya
   6. Nigeria, Ghana
   7. 41 million, 893 thousand
   8. South Africa; 49 million, 109 thousand

B. Answers will vary.

Page 28

A. 1. countries
   2. million
   3. Egypt
   4. Algeria
   5. Cairo
   6. Western Sahara
   7. Tunisia
   8. Mediterranean

Page 29

B. Students should color each country and region a different color.

Page 30

A. 1. No   6. No
   2. Yes   7. Yes
   3. No   8. No
   4. Yes   9. Yes
   5. Yes   10. Yes

Page 31

B. Answers will vary—e.g., Cape Verde is the only island nation in Western Africa.

Page 32

1. DRC
2. Middle Africa
3. São Tomé and Príncipe
4. Cameroon
5. Chad

Page 34

A. 1. h   5. d
   2. a   6. c
   3. g   7. e
   4. f   8. b

Page 35

B. Students should color Ethiopia, Madagascar, Seychelles, and Tanzania different colors. Then they should write one fact about each country.

Answers will vary—e.g.,
Ethiopia: largest country in both size and population
Madagascar: largest island nation
Seychelles: smallest island nation
Tanzania: second-largest country in both size and population

Page 36

B. 1. Namibia; Students should color Namibia yellow on page 37.
   2. Botswana; Students should color Botswana green on page 37.

Page 37

A.

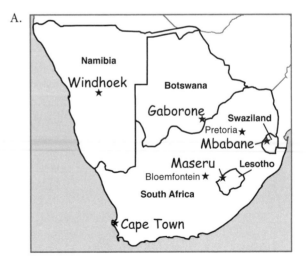

Page 39

A. 1. Lagos
2. less than 500,000
3. Kenya
4. Kano
5. three
6. Luanda
7. over 5 million
8. Senegal
9. three
10. Cape Town
11. Tanzania

B. first

Page 40

Across
2. second
7. Sudan
8. Nigeria

Down
1. billion
3. Eastern
4. country
5. island
6. Lagos

Page 43

1. B   2. C   3. A   4. B   5. D

Page 44

A. 1. Sahara
2. Mt. Kilimanjaro
3. eastern
4. Atlas
5. central
6. two-fifths
7. eastern
8. Madagascar

Page 45

B. Students should color the following:
Yellow: Sahara Desert, Kalahari Desert, Namib Desert
Green: Congo Basin
Orange: Great Rift Valley
Red: Horn of Africa
Brown: Atlas Mountains, Mount Kilimanjaro, Ethiopian Highlands

Page 47

A. 1. Yes
2. Yes
3. No
4. Yes
5. No
6. No
7. No
8. Yes
9. Yes
10. No

B. Students should color each zone a different color.

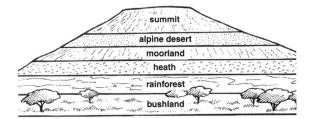

Page 49

1. Answers will vary—e.g., long with steep sides
2. salt
3. come together, move apart, or slide past each other
4. 112
5. Nubian and Somalian
6. The African Plate began to split apart, forming a fault.
7. It will split apart from the rest of Africa and become an island.

Page 51

A. 1. Sahara
2. Kalahari
3. Namib
4. Sahara
5. Namib
6. Kalahari
7. Sahara
8. Namib
9. Sahara
10. Kalahari

B. Answers will vary—e.g., Kalahari, because it has mild temperatures and receives plenty of rainfall.

Page 53

A. 1. savannas
2. seasons
3. continent
4. countries
5. grasses
6. baobab
7. Acacia
8. temperatures

B. Answers will vary—e.g.,
1. It stretches across the continent from the Atlantic to the Indian Ocean.
2. The grass grows very tall in the rainy season.
3. There are only two seasons: dry and rainy.
4. The acacia tree loses its leaves in the dry season.

Page 55

Students should color the rainforest areas three different colors and then complete the map key.
Rainforest Name
1. Western Africa   Color will vary.
2. Congo Basin   Color will vary.
3. Madagascar   Color will vary.

Page 57

1. largest
2. Mount
3. cyclones
4. rainforests
5. highlands
6. desert

Crack the Code!
Madagascar's nickname is the <u>Great Red Island</u>.

Page 59

A.

```
M D J U H D W A T L A N T I C
E E G J O N S A R B O Q A C H
D F N R V Y A E B C W P X R A
I G T N Y A S A K A B C D Z A
T V T A N G A N Y I K A A T R
E B C E A E P Q S A B M D A Z
R E Y R L J Q N A E B N U K A
R C A I B R C I P E C I D O M
A U N T E I R U Z E G N R C B
N E I G L O C I S A J D S K E
E F I M T G I W J B H I Q U Z
A N D C R H E C K D T A T O I
N R I D C O N G O C R N O I J
T V O W A E D I S L S E W N U
U I P K B T J N A R F I D S K
```

B. Answers will vary—e.g.,
1. The Nile River is the longest one in Africa.
2. There are two seas bordering the continent to the north.
3. The largest lake is Lake Victoria.

Page 61

1. Victoria	6. Victoria	11. Nyasa
2. Nyasa	7. Tanganyika	12. Victoria
3. Nyasa	8. Victoria	13. Nyasa
4. Tanganyika	9. Nyasa	14. Victoria
5. Nyasa	10. Tanganyika	

Page 63

A.
1. Nile	5. Niger
2. Zambezi	6. Nile
3. Niger	7. Congo
4. Congo	8. Zambezi

B.

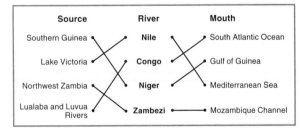

Page 65

A.
1. Yes	6. Yes
2. No	7. Yes
3. Yes	8. Yes
4. Yes	9. No
5. No	10. Yes

B. Students should label Victoria Falls between Zimbabwe and Zambia. Tugela Falls should be labeled near Lesotho.

Page 66

Across	Down
5. Tugela	1. Victoria
6. Sahara	2. Congo
7. Nile	3. Kilimanjaro
	4. savanna

Page 69

1. D   2. B   3. D   4. C   5. A

Page 71

A.
1. No	6. No
2. Yes	7. Yes
3. No	8. Yes
4. Yes	9. Yes
5. No	10. No

B. 1. 84,000,000 gallons
2. 318,000,000 liters
3. a gallon is about four times larger than a liter

Page 72

B. Students should color the following:
Yellow: Ghana, Mali, Tanzania
Blue: Botswana, Angola, Namibia
Yellow with blue stripes: DRC, South Africa

Page 73

A.
1. diamonds	6. Eighteen
2. Botswana	7. South Africa
3. gold	8. Africa
4. second	9. ore
5. thirty	10. Namibia

Page 75

A. 1. Yes   6. Yes
   2. No   7. No
   3. Yes   8. Yes
   4. No   9. No
   5. Yes   10. No

B. Answers will vary—e.g.,
   1. It saves money because they don't have to buy pesticides.
   2. It improves the soil.
   3. They can grow a variety of crops in the same field.

Page 77

A. 1. one-tenth
   2. 10
   3. Egypt and Sudan
   4. Mediterranean Sea
   5. the Nile River and all of the streams and rivers that flow into the Nile
   6. to find a way to share the Nile River as a source of water

B. Answers will vary—e.g.,
   1. electrical power
   2. drinking water

C. Students should color the Nile River blue and outline the surrounding basin in green on page 76.

Page 79

1. cacao
2. Ethiopia
3. leading
4. Uganda
5. beans
6. coffee

Crack the Code!
The average American eats 12 pounds (5.4 kg) of <u>chocolate</u> per year!

Page 80

1. Cape buffalo, elephant, leopard, lion, rhinoceros
2. Answers will vary—e.g., There is less hunting.
3. Answers will vary—e.g., People can study these wild animals in their natural habitat.

Page 83

A. 1. c   2. d   3. f   4. a   5. e   6. b

B. 1. 2 million
   2. wildebeest, zebras, gazelles
   3. lions, hyenas, cheetahs, leopards
   4. Answers will vary—e.g., starvation, dehydration, drowning, eaten by crocodiles

Page 85

A.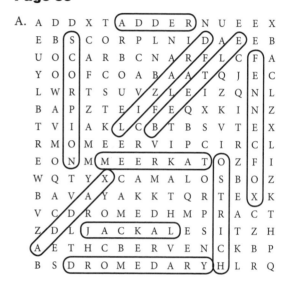

B. Answers will vary—e.g., Meercats are interesting, because they remind me of prairie dogs.

Page 87

A. 1. gorilla   5. gorilla
   2. lemur   6. mandrill
   3. mandrill   7. gorilla
   4. lemur   8. lemur

B. Drawings and captions will vary.

Page 88

Across	Down
3. cacao	1. diamonds
4. oil	2. wildebeest
7. Nile	5. gorilla
8. safaris	6. meercat

Page 91

1. A   2. D   3. B   4. C   5. C

Page 95

A.
1. pyramids
2. Giza
3. pharaoh
4. limestone
5. sarcophagus
6. King Khufu
7. King Menkaure
8. Great Sphinx
9. lion
10. King Khafre

B. Answers will vary—e.g., Yes, because they are old and mysterious.

Page 97

1. animal
2. ceremonies
3. leather
4. spear
5. soapstone
6. ebony
7. Human
8. museums
9. paint
10. bronze

Page 99

A. fabrics, mud, bogolon leaves, tree bark, calabash, meaning, story, health, white, geometric

B. 1. c   2. a   3. b

Page 101

1. response
2. piano
3. balafon
4. drum
5. kora
6. rhythms

Crack the Code!

In other parts of Africa, the sansa is called an <u>mbira</u>.

Page 103

A.
1. 2,000
2. 6
3. Niger-Congo
4. Swahili
5. Nilo-Saharan
6. Madagascar
7. Arabic and Berber
8. because many of the words are expressed with clicking sounds
9. Niger-Congo and Khoisan
10. English, French, Portuguese, Spanish

B. Students should use a different color on the map on page 102 for each language, and the key should match.

Page 105

A.
1. Yes
2. Yes
3. Yes
4. No
5. Yes
6. Yes
7. No
8. Yes
9. Yes
10. No

B.

Rank	Religion	Total Number of Followers	Percentage
1	Islam	370,872,000	45%
2	Christianity	304,000,000	37%
3	Traditional	138,000,000	17%

Page 107

A. 1. e   2. g   3. i   4. a   5. c
6. b   7. h   8. j   9. d   10. f

B. Answers will vary—e.g.,

Main Course	Description	Country
bobotie	meatloaf with raisins	South Africa
Second Course		
couscous	crushed, steamed grain	Morocco
Third Course		
dodo	fried plantains	Nigeria

Page 108

Across
5. languages
7. rhythms
8. dodo

Down
1. Islam
2. kente
3. pyramids
4. masks
6. Sphinx

Page 110

1. Sahara Desert
2. Nile River
3. Sudan
4. Mozambique Channel
5. Gulf of Guinea
6. Lake Victoria
7. Mount Kilimanjaro
8. Namibia
9. Madagascar
10. Cape Town

Page 111

1. C   2. A   3. D   4. B   5. D   6. A   7. B   8. C

Page 112

9. A   10. C   11. D   12. B   13. A   14. C   15. B   16. D

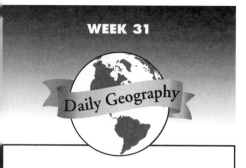

Skill: Cooperative Solutions
Essential Element 4: Standard 13

Time Zones of the United States

ANSWER KEY

Note: Not all questions can be answered with information from the map. Students will have to use their mental map skills to locate places on the map.

Monday
1. 6; Hawaiian-Aleutian, Alaskan, Pacific, Mountain, Central, and Eastern Times
2. one hour

Tuesday
1. earlier
2. Eastern Time

Wednesday
1. Hawaiian-Aleutian Time
2. 11:00 A.M.

Thursday
1. 10:00 P.M.
2. North Dakota, South Dakota, Nebraska, Kansas, and Texas

Friday
1. No, it's 2:00 A.M. and Grandfather is probably sleeping.
2. It is Daylight Saving Time.

Challenge
Answers will vary, but students should make up two questions and provide answers to the questions.

Introducing the Map

Ask students what it would be like if every community in the United States used a different time. The obvious answer is that people would be confused and many problems would be created. To avoid this confusion, a cooperative system was designed called *standard time zones*. Talk about the advantages of having regional time zones.

Explain the concept of time zones. A day is 24 hours long—the time it takes Earth to complete one rotation on its axis. Earth is divided into 24 time zones. The United States is divided into six of those twenty-four time zones.

Show students the Time Zones of the United States map. Tell students that each zone uses a time one hour different from its neighboring zones. The hours are earlier to the west of each zone and later to the east.

Go over all the names of the time zones and have students notice the one hour difference between each of them. Talk about how Alaska is so large that it covers two time zones. Explain that some of the Aleutian Islands of Alaska are so far west that scientists placed them with Hawaii, thus creating Hawaiian-Aleutian Time.

Ask students which time zone Chicago, Illinois, is in. They will probably say Central Time. Then ask them: If it is 3:00 P.M. in Chicago, what time is it in Denver? The answer is 2:00 P.M. Ask students a couple more questions, each time changing the local times to help students understand the concept.

Extend the lesson to discuss daylight saving time. This is a plan in which clocks are set one hour ahead of standard time for a certain period of time. The plan provides for an additional hour of daylight. It begins on the first Sunday in April and ends on the last Sunday in October. Most states choose to go on daylight saving time, but several don't. Talk about how that complicates things.

Introducing Vocabulary

daylight saving time a plan in which clocks are set one hour ahead of standard time for a specific period of time

standard time zone a region in which the same time is used

time zone a region in which the same time is used; Earth is divided into 24 time zones

Time Zones of the United States

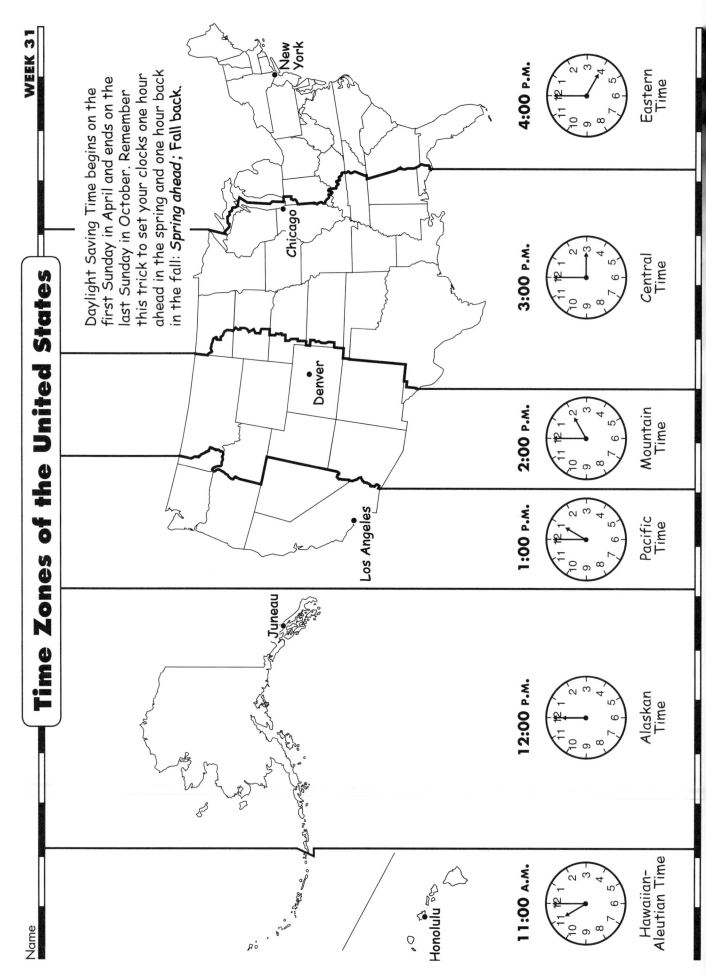

Daylight Saving Time begins on the first Sunday in April and ends on the last Sunday in October. Remember this trick to set your clocks one hour ahead in the spring and one hour back in the fall: *Spring ahead; Fall back.*

4:00 P.M. Eastern Time

3:00 P.M. Central Time

2:00 P.M. Mountain Time

1:00 P.M. Pacific Time

12:00 P.M. Alaskan Time

11:00 A.M. Hawaiian–Aleutian Time

Name _____

Time Zones of the United States

Monday

1. The United States is divided into how many standard time zones? Name them from west to east.

   _____

   _____

   _____

2. What is the time difference between each neighboring time zone?

   _____

Tuesday

1. Are the hours earlier or later to the west of each time zone?

   _____

2. Cities in the Northeast region are part of which time zone?

   _____

Wednesday

1. Which time zone includes Hawaii and some of the western islands of Alaska?

   _____

2. If it is 1:00 P.M. in Chicago, what time is it in Los Angeles?

   _____

Time Zones of the United States

Thursday

1. If it is midnight in Chicago, what time is it in Seattle, Washington?

   _____

2. Which states have areas that are part of Central and Mountain Time Zones?

   _____

   _____

   _____

Friday

1. If you live in Honolulu and it is 9:00 P.M., is it a good time to call your grandfather in New York? Why or why not?

   _____

   _____

2. It is the first Sunday in April and clocks have been set one hour ahead. Why?

   _____

Challenge

Make up two time zone questions. Write your questions on the back of the map. Don't forget to include the answer. Pair up with a classmate and ask each other the time zone questions.